CW01084228

Handel's Path to Covent Garden

E. A. Bucchianeri

Batalha Publishers
Maxieira, Portugal

Hardcover, Second Edition 2010
ISBN: 978-989-96844-3-0

Library of Congress Subject Headings

Bucchianeri, E.A.
    Handel's Path to Covent Garden
    Bibliography
    Includes index.
    1. Covent Garden (London, England)—History. 2. Handel, George Frideric, 1685-1759. 3. Handel, George Frideric, 1685-1759. Operas. 4. Opera—England—18th century.

British Library Subject Headings

Bucchianeri, E.A.
    Handel's Path to Covent Garden
    1. Covent Garden—(London, England)— History. 2. Handel, George Frideric, 1685-1759, Operas. 3. Opera—England—London—18th Century

Books by the same author:

A Compendium of Essays:
Purcell, Hogarth and Handel, Beethoven, Liszt, Debussy,
and Andrew Lloyd Webber

Faust: My Soul be Damned for the World

Out of the ashes the Phoenix rises.

Table of Contents

Chapter 3

Chapter 4

Chapter 5

An Addendum: Independence and Expectations

Appendices

Introduction

George Frideric Handel's career as an Italian opera composer in England was fraught with many adversities and he was frequently forced to confront countless difficulties and irritations. The first manifestations of these problems emerged when Italians influenced by the Arcadian Academy in Italy attempted to usurp the English cultural scene and supplant their own ideals of reformed Italian opera in London during the early 1700s. When the Royal Academy was established in 1719, Handel encountered a myriad of challenges with this particular circle, which had been reinforced by the arrival of additional influential Arcadians, notably the difficulties with the castrato Francesco Bernardi ("Senesino"), the competition from the composer Giovanni Bononcini, and most importantly, the antagonism of the librettist Paolo Rolli who had previously arrived in 1715. A conflict in ideals escalated and permeated the entire Academy, thereby creating numerous altercations between the directors, composers, singers, subscribers, and their supporters.

Handel's greatest challenges were yet to emerge when the Royal Academy collapsed in 1728 as the popularity for Italian opera in London waned and the desire for an English style of opera waxed stronger. During this time, Handel remained undaunted by this unorthodox chain of events and entered into a partnership with John Jacob Heidegger, the manager of the King's Theatre in the Haymarket, for the next four to five years, whereby he persisted with his personal ambitions for the production of Italian opera. In 1733, the nobility formed a rival opera company with Rolli and Senesino in competition with Handel, recognised today as the Opera of the Nobility. In 1734, when their business obligation concluded, Heidegger leased the King's Theatre to the new opera company; as a result of Heidegger's action, Handel entered into a venture with John Rich at Covent Garden and remained there until 1737 struggling with the competition from the Opera of the Nobility company. Finally, both ventures collapsed as the public's support splintered between the two rival theatres.

We may regard the 1730s as the most trying decade of Handel's career; unfortunately, this period became obscured through time and speculation, therefore many questions have remained unanswered. To enable us to comprehend this era, it is necessary for us to explore the important issues and subsequent circumstances that effected his transfer to Covent Garden in 1734. We may question what initially prompted Handel to relocate to Covent Garden. Did his past experiences at the Royal Academy set the pattern for future obstacles and confrontations that he was compelled to contend with during the 1730s? Perhaps many of the difficulties Handel encountered with Rolli and his Italian circle of friends and supporters perpetuated similar disturbances later in Handel's career. This may be the key to answer many of the questions relating to Handel's relocation, and may explain his progressive and creative innovations displayed within his operas from this period.

My primary objectives of this study are: to determine what initiated these difficulties, establish how and when the problems and related issues presented themselves, and attempt to interpret the influences they exerted on Handel's opera career during the 1730s, in particular, his first Covent Garden term from 1734–1737. Apparently, these problems gradually emerged and progressed as time and events unfolded. My philosophical research and observations pertaining to this current study have presented themselves sequentially. Therefore, the logical procedure is to examine and present all the major issues and related facts in chronological order, concluding with a brief review of Handel's career in Covent Garden. I hope by using this method of deduction, the challenges encountered by Handel during the 1720s and 1730s may be effectively illustrated, thereby clarifying the circumstances concerning his relocation to Covent Garden.

Acknowledgements:

I would like to express my sincere gratitude to Dr. Ellen T. Harris and Dr. Reinhard Strohm. Throughout the course of my research, they graciously corresponded and offered assistance.

I am also indebted to the Handelian scholars whose work and previous research contributed significantly to this philosophical study of Handel's path to Covent Garden.

Editorial Policy:

The format of the various quotes, i.e. punctuation, spellings and italics, have been preserved unless otherwise stated. For the sake of clarity, quotes from John Mainwaring's biography of Handel containing the letter 's' spelled as 'f' in Old English have been altered. Where no translations of foreign language texts have been offered, I have taken the liberty of translating them as accurately as possible myself; these passages will be indicated. Italics that I have inserted have been indicated, and/or should be clear from the context. Ellipses, including those within brackets, [...], or parentheses, (...), have been inserted by other authors, e.g. if ellipses form part of a quote taken from a secondary source. Ellipses or observations inserted within braces, e.g. {...}, indicate my own observations and editing. Dates have been given as they stand in the sources, English primary sources are in the Old Style. Dates given after the title of an opera or similar work generally refer to a premiere, unless reference to a specific production is intended, which should be clear from the context.

Chapter 1

The Demand for Italian Opera in London
and the Creation of the Rival Factions

John Mainwaring in his important biography of Handel lauds the days of the Royal Academy as "a period of musical glory" — not many would argue with this description.[1] In 1719, the Royal Academy was founded by members of the British aristocracy to provide London with Italian opera on a permanent basis with a secure financial foundation; previously, Italian opera had floundered in England, as this form of entertainment was an expensive novelty to maintain and did not enjoy assured financial protection. With the advent of these new "secure" days, London became one of the greatest opera centres of Europe and could boast of having the most renowned composers and singers in the world at its disposal. During this time, Handel's operas achieved phenomenal success; undoubtedly it was a period of musical glory for Handel where Italian opera was concerned.

However, Mainwaring paints a cloud upon this description in his next paragraph; he declares in so many words, the Academy was doomed from the very beginning like all finite objects in that the seeds of its dissolution were carried within from its very inception.[2] Mainwaring asserted the timing of the eventual closure of such a venture depends on those who impede the inevitable, or further its outcome. This is a rather dramatic and philosophical perception of the Academy's demise, yet it is one perception that obviously

---

[1] John Mainwaring, *Memoirs of the Life of the Late George Frederic Handel* (London: R. And J. Dodsley, in *Pall Mall*, 1760). Reprint, (New York: Da Capo Press Music Reprint Series, 1980), p.106.

[2] Ibid. pp. 106–107.

requires further exploration. Did Handel unwittingly contribute to the demise of the Royal Academy or was he attempting to delay the inevitable? Could Handel have prevented the closure of the Royal Academy and thereby avert the forthcoming problems that resulted with his relocation to Covent Garden?

In an attempt to address these questions, it is important to ascertain if the Academy was truly doomed from its inception as Mainwaring suggests. Noticeably, Mainwaring concentrates on the *personal* factors behind the scenes that caused the friction, i.e. the quarrels between the directors, singers, and composers. True, the financial management and the day-to-day administration of the company created its own consequences, yet other circumstances could have determined the closure of such an enterprise. What exactly were the motivations of the administrators or regulators who worked or participated within the Academy? Different viewpoints vigorously defended whether they are correct or incorrect have often resulted with the termination of lifelong friendships and business partnerships.

A similar observation may be applied to the various factions that developed within the Academy. In Otto Erich Deutsch's documentary biography a hostile party opposing Handel within the Academy is apparent; particularly within the various surviving letters of the Italian librettist Paolo Rolli.[3] Subsequently in his book, Mainwaring, in describing the rival group in opposition to Handel during the 1730s, i.e. the Opera of the Nobility, relates that it was an Italian orientated clique.[4] Mainwaring was obviously fascinated

---

[3] These letters are reprinted in Otto Erich Deutsch's book, *Handel; a Documentary Biography* (New York: Da Capo Press, 1974). Reprint of the 1955 edition, (New York: W.W. Norton).

[4] Mainwaring offers this comment concerning the formation of the Opera of the Nobility and the skill of one of their composers, Hasse; "He is remarkable for his fine elevated air, with hardly so much as the shew of harmony to support it. And this may serve not only for a character of Hasse — in particular, but of the Italians in general, at the time we are

with the idea that a hostile party besieged Handel; however, there may be some grain of truth to his observation. Handel's friend, Johann Mattheson, wrote this account relating Handel's difficulties of the 1730s:

> Once a report had it that, on account of the Italian spite and persecution, he was at the end of his tether. That was shortly before the time when, as mentioned before, *he instanced me of his unfortunate circumstances.*[5]

This quote raises additional questions requiring further investigation. Did this Italian faction facilitate the downfall of the Royal Academy and consequently precipitate Handel's difficulties of the 1730s? Why were they resistant to Handel who was partial to Italian *opera seria* in the first instance? What actions did Handel take to have provoked such irritation? Perhaps Handel resisted them for a particular reason. What instigated such aggravation in this noble organisation? Who sowed the "seeds of dissolution" within the Academy?

We observe it is important to determine when and why these factions materialised, and to accomplish this we need to understand the circumstances that initiated this rivalry. Generally, it may be stated that a new group or society is founded to provide a necessary service or to carry out an objective, and in order to secure a viable organisation, it would be necessary for the members to reach an agreement whereby they would comply with a focused agenda. In

---

speaking of. The opposition in which they were engaged against Handel, made him look upon that merit in his antagonists with much indifference, and upon this defect with still more contempt." Mainwaring, pp. 117–118.

[5] Johann Mattheson, "Grundlage Einer Ehren–Pforte," (Hamburg, 1740.) Quoted in Deutsch, p. 505. The letter of Handel that Mattheson was referring to was written in July, 1735.

this instance, the Royal Academy was established to produce opera; however, it is possible that a clash of ideals was the main cause of discord if the various members of the Royal Academy developed their own singular plans for the organisation and they failed to comply with a definite agenda or policy.

Surprisingly, it would seem these factions emerged very early, i.e. before and during the time of Handel's arrival in 1710. While it may appear futile to examine the series of events dating from the pre-Academy days, Handel's future problems had their foundations set during the years 1705–1719. When Italian opera was initially introduced to England, the Italians present in London endeavoured to subdue English attempts at developing their own style of opera. The ideology encompassing opera culture in London fluctuated as these developments took effect; therefore, many opera enthusiasts entertained varying and conflicting opinions on what they anticipated of opera. This public perception would affect the foundation of the Royal Academy in 1719; therefore, it is essential to review the major highlights of this early period.

In 1705, Italian opera was introduced to London audiences through the work *Arsinoe* that was originally set by Petronio Franceschini and produced in 1677.[6] This London version featured a text entirely in English and the music was composed with the collaboration of three different composers: Thomas Clayton, Nicolino Haym, and Charles Dieupart.[7] Eric Walter White states that the production of operatic genres was inevitable, as there were many superb foreign and domestic singers present in London at that time.[8] White surmised they may have desired the opportunity to

---

[6] Eric Walter White, *A History of English Opera* (London: Faber and Faber Ltd., BAS Printers Ltd., 1983), p. 140.

[7] Ibid. p. 140.

[8] These singers were Signora Maria Lindelheim, who had learned to sing in Italy, Francesca Margarita de l'Epine, and her sister Maria Margarita Gallia. There was also Mrs. Catherine Tofts, an English singer known for performing Italian and English songs who was in direct

perform in an opera as their principal performances consisted of singing songs for concerts in the various theatres; naturally, Italian opera proved to be the obvious model for this undertaking.[9]

However, evidence suggests the opera *Arsinoe* was initially intended to serve as an example of what could be accomplished to further the progress of *English* music. Primarily, the cast was English, also, Clayton in his preface to the libretto of *Arsinoe* wrote:

> The design of this entertainment being to introduce the Italian manner of musick on the English stage, which has not been before attempted; I was oblig'd to have an Italian opera translated; In which the words, however mean in several places, suited much better with that manner of musick, than others more poetical would do. The stile of this music is to express the passions, which is the soul of the musick; And though the voices are not equal to the Italian, yet I have engag'd the best that were to be found in England, and I have not been wanting, to the utmost of my diligence, in the instructing of them. The musick being recitative, may not, at first, meet with that general acceptation as is hop'd for from the audience's being better acquainted with it; But if this attempt shall, by pleasing the nobility and gentry, *be a means of bringing this manner of music to be use'd by in my native country,*[*] I shall think all my study and pains very well employ'd.[10]

Obviously, the primary goal of this endeavour was to introduce only the *manner* of Italian music into England. It was the introduction of recitative that Clayton hoped would prove

---

competition with Margarita de l'Epine. Ibid. pp. 138–139.

[9] Ibid. p. 140.

[*] Italics added.

[10] Ibid. pp. 140–141.

successful, adding that all his work would have been rewarded if the English were willing to adopt the convention of recitative upon hearing *Arsinoe*. Therefore, we may venture that although this work is regarded as the first introduction of Italian opera to London audiences, it was intended to serve an alternative purpose. Perhaps *Arsinoe* was designed as an example of what the English could accomplish with respect to their native dramatic genres and develop what Henry Purcell had achieved with his semi-operas?

There are other examples that may prove the Italian operas introduced were intended to further the cause for English opera. The following operas also featured English texts adapted from the original Italian sources: *The Loves of Ergasto* (April 1705), *The Temple of Love* (March 1706), and *Camilla* (March 1706).[11] An additional attempt to improve English opera occurred with the production of *Rosamond* (March 1707). It was predominately English and composed "after the Italian Manner"; Joseph Addison wrote the libretto and the music was composed by Clayton. [12] Apparently, Clayton was following his own council from his prologue of *Arsinoe* by attempting to continue the introduction of the Italian style he had initiated through *Rosamond*. Sadly, this venture was a failure and lasted for only three performances; had this work succeeded, the history of English opera may have been changed.[13]

Unfortunately, it would appear the design to introduce Italian opera as a medium to reform English genres had backfired. One of the primary reasons for this failure was the increasing number of Italian singers arriving in London; obviously, audiences began to appreciate the Italian style of singing when heard with the

---

[11] Ibid. p. 141.

[12] Ibid. p. 142.

[13] Merril Knapp attributes the failure of this work to the lack of quality in Clayton's music and the weak English adaptation of the plot. See Merril Knapp, 'A Forgotten Chapter in English Eighteenth-Century Opera,' *Music and Letters* Vol. XLII (1961): p. 5.

original Italian language. [14]   When the castrato Valentini Urbano
arrived from Italy in December of 1707, producers altered the text
of *Camilla*, thereby making it possible for him to perform his verses
in Italian. [15] Apparently, this change secured the success of *Camilla*,
although this motley half-bred result in the dialogue created
confusion.   Valentini sang in a similar fashion in other English-
translated operas such as *Thomyris, Queen of Scythia* (April, 1707)
and *Love's Triumph* (1708). [16] Valentini would be joined later by
the celebrated castrato Nicolo Grimaldi, ('Nicolini'), in 1708.
Nicolini's first London appearance was in *Pyrrhus and Demetrius*
(December, 1708); he performed in Italian with Valentini while
Mrs. Tofts and the other ladies sang in English. [17] Nicolini was a
phenomenal success, and audiences acclaimed his skills as an actor.

Having experienced these singers perform in their native
language, English audiences now wished to hear Italian opera as it
was originally composed featuring the Italian language and musical
style. They evidently misunderstood the intentions concerning the
translation of Italian operas into English, and the endeavor to
reform and produce English operas using the Italian format as
Cibber's comment illustrates:

> {...} the *Italian* Opera began first to steal into
> *England*, but in a rude disguise, and unlike itself as
> possible; in a lame, hobbling Translation into our own
> Language, with false Quantities, or Metre out of
> Measure to its original Notes, sung by our own
> unskilled Voices, with Graces misapply'd to almost
> every Sentiment, and with Action lifeless and
> unmeaning through every Character, {...} [18]

---

[14] See f. 8, regarding the Italian singers already present in London.
[15] White, *English Opera*, p. 142.
[16] Ibid. pp. 143.
[17] Ibid. p. 145.
[18] Ed. Robert W. Low, "An Apology for the Life of Mr. Colley

Other circumstances may have facilitated this misunderstanding with the public. For instance, there were additional attempts at introducing Italian opera to further the cause of English opera development, as we observe with Aaron Hill's intentions concerning Handel's opera *Rinaldo* of 1711:

> Nor shall I then be longer doubtful of succeeding in my Endeavour, to see the *English* OPERA more splendid than her MOTHER the Italian. [19]

However, they undermined their own efforts by creating operas with greater emphasis on the Italianate style. In hindsight, we may perceive they inadvertently erred; alternatively, they could have perfected the flaws experienced in the past as with *Rosamond* by producing new operas emphasising a distinctive Anglican style. Hill's preface in the wordbook for *Rinaldo* clearly illustrates his well-intentioned miscalculations. (See Appendix One.) Hill's solution to the awkward Anglican endeavours was to improve the Italian model and thereby construct a satisfactory example for the English. *However, he may have created a demand for authentic Italian opera.* True, the English translated operas may not appear as skillfully composed when compared with their Italian originals, yet again we can argue that an authentic reproduction of Italian opera may not have been intended. Notwithstanding the commendable endeavours to improve English opera, they continued to highlight the deficiencies perceived with the English translated operas by perpetuating this method of adopting the Italian model for reformational purposes. Hill had provided for the lack of a complete Italian text through his collaboration with Rossi and thereby had

---

Cibber," (London: 1889), in Merril Knapp; 'A Forgotten Chapter,' p. 5.

[19] From Hill's dedication to Queen Anne in the wordbook of *Rinaldo*, in Deutsch, p. 32.

rectified the "hobbling Translation" stated by Cibber with "Words so sounding and rich in Sense" as Hill himself described. Elaborate stage machinery had also been employed which enhanced the novelty of the production. Of paramount significance, Handel composed the music incorporating the skills he had recently absorbed in Italy; to the aural perception of the London audiences, this musical experience must have been astounding, and as a result, the earlier English attempts of setting music to the Italian model were revealed as pale shadows in comparison. Under these circumstances, the public's enthusiasm to embrace Italian opera is comprehensible.

However, other composers endeavoured to amend the misunderstandings that resulted from adopting the Italian format, ironically, by producing additional English operas based on the Italian model. For instance, one particularly important attempt at composing an English opera should be mentioned. The opera in question is *Calypso and Telemachus;* it was produced in May 1712 with text by John Huges and music by John Erst Galliard. [20] (Incidentally, Handel had returned to Germany at this point.) We notice they contrived this opera to rectify the misconceptions entertained by the English when observing a section of Huges' preface to the printed libretto; notice in particular the first and last paragraphs of the quoted example:

> The following OPERA is an Essay for the Improvement of Theatrical Music in the *English* Language, after the Model of the *Italians.*
>
> It is certain, that this Art has for a considerable time florish'd in *Italy* in greater Perfection than in any other Country. As the *Grecians* were formerly the Masters in Architecture, Sculpture, Painting and Musick, whose Rules and Examples were follow'd by

---

[20] Knapp, 'A Forgotten Chapter,' p. 7.

other Nations, the *Italians* are generally allow'd to be so now. It is some Years that Musick of our Theatre has been almost wholly supply'd by them. Their most celebrated *Opera's* have been introduc'd among us, and a generous Encouragement has been given to such as came over, and perform'd Parts in them on the *English* Stage. By this means the Entertainments of *Italy* are become familiar to us, and our Audiences have heard the finest Compositions and Performances of *Rome* and *Venice*, without trouble of travelling to those Places.

I am not of the Opinion of those who impute this Encouragement given to *Italian* Musick, to an Affectation of every thing that is Foreign.

I wou'd rather ascribe it to the ingenuous Temper of the *British* Nation, that they are willing to be instructed in so elegant an Art by the best Examples. But after this Justice done to others, there is likewise a Justice due to our selves. It cou'd never have been the Intention of those, who first promoted the *Italian* Opera, that it shou'd take the intire [*sic*] Possession of our Stage, to the Exclusion of every thing of the like kind, which might be produc'd here. This wou'd be to suppress that Genius which Foreigners so commonly applaud in the *English*, who if they are not always the Inventors of Arts, are yet allow'd to be no ill Learners, and are often observ'd to improve that Knowledge, which they first receiv'd from others. {...}[21]

Calypso and Telemachus, like *Rosamond*, would be ill fated to have a short life; it had four performances with three more revivals in 1717.[22] Obviously, this opera was produced too late as *Rinaldo* had already swept the public away; perhaps if they had

---

[21] Ibid. pp. 10–11.
[22] Ibid. p. 7.

produced *Calypso* before *Rinaldo,* the message contained in the libretto preface may have been acted upon at an earlier date.

This attempt to correct the "Italian opera controversy" did not create the desired result, however, the English refused to retreat from the operatic scene. The obvious short-term solution until this issue could be resolved was to return to the English masters of the past; the reopening of the Lincoln's-Inn-Fields theatre in November 1714 ushered in a revival of Purcell's works.[23] There was a concert performance of *Dioclesian* in 1712, and was produced again from 1715 to 1718.[24] In 1715 and 1716, *The Island Princess* and select excerpts of music from *King Arthur* were performed, while in 1715 *The Indian Queen* and *Bonduca* were also revived.[25] In addition, other early English operas were produced such as *Macbeth* and *The Tempest.*[26] Concurrently, a renewed interest for theatrical masque developed while several of the earlier attempts figuring bilingual operas were revived such as *Camilla, Thomyris,* and *Calypso and Telemachus* as mentioned previously, in 1717. The quest to establish a national opera style had not vanished completely.

However, these attempts would not avert what had already been initiated; a rival faction had rallied in opposition to the English cause resulting in the embryonic formation of future conflicting factions. As we have observed, the English had planned to use the influential Italian singers who were present and their style of opera to further their own ambitions, however, it would appear the Italian performers and those affiliated with them developed their own agenda. This group, the "Italian circle" as George Dorris refers to them,[27] were apprehensive that these experiments with English opera

---

[23] For more information concerning which theatres produced the revivals, see White, *English Opera*, pp. 170–171.

[24] Ibid. p. 171.

[25] Ibid.

[26] Ibid.

[27] George E. Dorris, *Paolo Rolli and the Italian Circle in London* (The Hague: Mounton and Co., 1967), op. cit.

would be in direct competition with the fledgling Italian opera in England; they may also have been annoyed with the "mutilation" of their operas.

Strikingly, the English production of *Calypso and Telemachus* had more to contend with than the misfortune of its production occurring after *Rinaldo*. Apparently, this clique devised a despicable plot to foil *Calypso*, for it was reported they had approached the Lord Chamberlain, the Duke of Shrewsbury, to remove the subscription for this opera and to have the theatre opened at the lowest prices if he could not close it down completely. [28] The Italian circle was closely associated with the nobility, and with these powerful patrons and their support, they could promote the cause for their own opera; this is one example of how they could exert their influence.

The Gathering of the Italian Circle in London:
The Arcadian Academy and its Influential Members

Subsequent to the formation of the Italian circle an "invasion" had been launched which would prove troublesome to the operatic scene in England for future decades. Surprisingly, this artistic revolution was concerned with the cause of literature rather than music aesthetics; many influential members of the Italian clique in London were part of, or were in connection with the Arcadian Academy, a society that had been established in Rome to reform Italian literature. [29] It is important for us to understand this movement and how it affected the opera culture of London as consequently it influenced Handel's work.

The Academy first developed with the *letterati* who

---

[28] Knapp, 'A Forgtten Chapter,' p. 7.

[29] Dorris, *Italian Circle*, pp. 27–30.

assembled at the salon of Queen Christina of Sweden during the latter half of the seventeenth century, and was formally instituted in 1690.[30] Their intention was to reform Italian literature through simplicity and tranquillity symbolised by the pastoral life based upon the style of Virgil rather than a realistic ideal.[31] Isadore Carini states that:

> This was not an academy of mere poetry, but rather an eclectic gathering of the learned, devoted to every branch of human knowledge, brought together only in this: to reclaim good taste in Italy, where it was running to madness; to impede the announcement of great truths in insipid and rude language; to place honour over every other thing the art of giving form to thought; and to join the amenity of style and the adornment of the word to the real historical, moral, physical, and mathematical disciplines; a purpose, as is clearly apparent, nobler than any other.[32]

Apparently, Italian theatrical drama was virtually nonexistent in the latter part of the seventeenth century and this encouraged the Arcadian reform movement.[33] During this period, spoken drama was performed in a select number of centres and academies in the major cities of Italy as in Rome, Parma, Modena, Bologna, Sienna and Florence.[34] Pier Jacopo Martelli, Gian-Vicenza Gravina, and Scipione Maffei initiated attempts to establish a national theatrical

---

[30] Ibid. p. 27.

[31] Ibid. pp. 27–28.

[32] Isadore Carini, 'L' Arcadia dal 1690 al 1890' (Roma: 1891): pp. 46–47 in Dorris, *Italian Circle*, p. 30.

[33] Dorris, *Italian Circle*, p. 31.

[34] Reinhard Strohm, *Dramma per Musica: Italian Opera Seria of the Eighteenth Century* (New Haven, London: Yale University Press, 1997), p. 4.

style in collaboration with Luigi Riccoboni, yet they had no affect in promoting this purpose. The popularity of Italian *dramma per musica*[35] had eclipsed all these efforts towards spoken drama; alternatively, this genre had achieved the status of a national art form as Reinhard Strohm points out:

> {...} Nevertheless, the *dramma per musica* in eighteenth-century Italy had the cultural significance of a national art-form. Italian opera was capable of suggesting a national unity which in political terms seemed unattainable. It inherited much of the aura *of italianità* which the Italian language and poetry had possessed since the times of Petrarch.[36]

As a result, major reforms centred on Italian *opera seria* — reformists perceived opera as the most deplorable form of theatrical drama as they believed it had been subject to "corruptive elements". Their goal was to establish refinement within the arts by imitating the true traditions of classical tragedy, according to their interpretation.[37] Their theories were derived from the philosophy of Aristotle and his conception of drama as subsequently developed by Pierre Corneille.[38]

Drama was categorised into six sections descending in order of importance: (1) fable, (2) ethos, (3) pathos, (4) diction, (5) music, (6) and scenography. Frequently, the reformists regarded

---

[35] Dorris, *Italian Circle*, p. 32. Also, Strohm, *Dramma per Musica*, p. 4. Spoken comedies were more successful, but still could not compete with the popularity of opera. Ibid.

[36] Strohm, *Dramma per Musica*, p. 5.

[37] Ibid. p. 122.

[38] Pierre Corneille, 'Trois discours sur le poème dramatique (1660)' from P. Corneille, *Œuvres complètes*, vol. 3, ed. by Georges Counton (Paris: Gallimard, 1987), pp. 117–90, 123–34, in Strohm, *Dramma per Musica*, p. 17.

music as the most corrupt element and thereby listed it as the last category during this period.[39] Resulting from this perception, opera was considered a deviation from classical tradition. Strohm quotes Enrico Fubini concerning the contemporary view regarding music within *opera seria*:

> But the degeneration was already contained *in nuce* in the genre of opera itself, from the very first appearance: music inevitably corroded its dramatic aspirations from its roots; it encroached on it as an element of disturbance, as a certain feeling, unexplainable under the light of reason, and unacceptable on the theatrical stage.[40]

The Arcadians were dissatisfied with opera for in their opinion it failed to conform to the ideal of Aristotelian verisimilitude. Strohm neatly pinpoints the problem these reformists associated with opera:

> The main conflict arose, of course, from the singing of arias. Singing on stage is reputed to be improbable in classicist theory (it contradicts Nature), especially in tragedy, which prefers heroic and historical plots and characters. In Italian opera the 'reform' librettos of the period around 1700, by increasingly adopting such plots, created a contradiction: according to theory, gods and shepherds were allowed to sing arias, but Alexander or Julius Caesar were not. This type of problem had already surfaced a century earlier:

---

[39] Strohm, *Dramma per Musica*, p. 239.

[40] Enrico Fubini, 'Razionalità e irrazionalità in Metastasio,' from *Metastasio e il melodrama*, ed. by Elena Sala di Felice and Laura Sannia Nowé (Padua: Liviana editrice, 1985): pp. 39–53, in Strohm, *Dramma per Musica*, p. 271.

orthodox Aristotelians, judging from the viewpoint of verisimilitude, condemned not only singing but even speaking in verse on the tragic stage.[41]

Therefore, we are not surprised to observe that the Arcadians concentrated significantly on the reformation of opera librettos. Giovanni Maria Crescimbeni had drastic proposals for operatic reformation as Strohm relates:

> He advocated the return to the aesthetic of the *favole pastorali* with their pastoral setting (i.e. without change of scenery except for *macchine*), simple conflict (*nodo semplice*), few arias and much recitative, and choruses. The first two suggestions were at least extremely restrictive for the stage, {…}. The last two suggestions were particularly far-reaching as they affected the business of the composer — without mentioning him. [42]

Crescimbeni praised others such as Apostolo Zeno who complied with the practise of diminishing the number of arias and placing greater emphasis on the recitatives in his librettos.[43] Incidentally, the librettists Paolo Rolli and Metastasio were influenced by Zeno's reforms.[44]

Pietro Metastasio, recognised as one of the finest librettists of Italian *opera seria*, advocated these ideals and remained in firm opposition to the inclusion of music in the genre of opera. He also

---

[41] Strohm, *Dramma per Musica*, pp. 202–203.

[42] Ibid. p. 123.

[43] Ibid.

[44] Dorris, *Italian Circle*, p. 129. Zeno's influence is important to note as Rolli was one of the major figures behind the operatic scene in London, and Metastasio's librettos would become prominent in the 1730s. These points shall be examined later.

endorsed claims by contemporary critics who maintained the words should have greater importance than the music, thereby rendering the drama more intelligible, and/or to achieve expressive compatibility between the two elements.[45] His unparalleled success with librettos appears to be his development of the concept that 'arias = emotion' and 'recitative = action' as a method to breech the barriers separating music and verisimilitude.[46]

The Arcadian scholar Ludovico Antonio Muratori also expressed his opposition to operatic music corresponding with Fubini's observations concerning the aesthetics of the time.[47] Muratori had considerable influence for he was perceived as a "fixed point of reference" for those who were endeavouring to progress Italian letters in Italy and in other countries.[48]

Resulting from these efforts, Italian dramatists concentrated primarily on the poetry of opera, as they attempted to assimilate opera into a dramatic literary genre by purging and suppressing its musical aspect. The librettists directed the rehearsals, not the composer,[49] and it has been suggested recitatives were on occasions delegated to composition students.[50] When a new production was commissioned, frequently the recitatives were newly composed while individual arias were reused and copied.[51] Obviously, these conventions give precedence to the drama, diminishing the role of

---

[45] Strohm, *Drama per Musica*, p. 25.

[46] Ibid. p. 203.

[47] Ibid. pp. 123, 271.

[48] Dorris, *Italian Circle*, p. 26. Through the surviving letters written by the Modenese diplomat Riva to members of the Arcadian Academy, such as Muratori, (which are reproduced in Deutsch's documentary of Handel), we observe how the Arcadians viewed the operatic scene in London.

[49] Reinhard Strohm, 'Metastasio's Alessandro nell'Indie and its earliest settings,' *Essay's on Handel and Italian Opera* (Great Britain: Cambridge University Press, 1985), p. 234. Also Strohm, *Drama per musica*, p. 10.

[50] Strohm, *Drama per musica*, p. 10.

[51] Ibid. p. 11.

the composer and his musical contribution to the genre. Could this possibly explain why the principal singers of a company were regarded with great esteem? They were perceived as the reciters of the poetic texts and as such were granted significant artistic freedom. [52] The availability of singers influenced the decisions regarding the subject of the text — not only were their roles customised, frequently whole operas were constructed to accommodate their individual personalities and skills. In addition, singers had considerable freedom of expression with the *da capo* aria where it was conventional for them to perform improvised ornamentation. Notably, they also had a personal repertory of arias, *arie di baule*, and upon their request, selections from this source were included in the opera.[53]

Clearly it is evident no particular status was directed towards the composer's participation in the creation of an opera. Under these circumstances, the concept of a unified work, i.e. an equal relationship between music, drama, and scenography as we have become accustomed to expect of opera today in *Gesamtkunstwerk* fashion did not apply. These conventions would result in future problems for England, particularly with Handel's career and the formation of the Royal Academy.

The Members of the Italian Circle in London

In addition to centring their reforms in Italy, this Arcadian movement had extended its influence to other European cities, as in Paris and Vienna; the Arcadians were attempting to re-establish Italian dominance in art and literature which had been lost to France during the seventeenth century.[54] *Opera seria* was perceived as a

---

[52] Strohm, 'Towards an Understanding of the opera seria,' *Essays*, pp. 97–99.

[53] Strohm, *Drama per Musica*, p. 11.

[54] Dorris, *Italian Circle*, p. 11.

national genre in Italy as previously mentioned, therefore it seemed the obvious medium to employ despite their reservations regarding this "corrupted" genre.

London would now become the next important conquest of the Arcadian "colonisation campaign". We have already discussed the arrival of the first "settlers" in the previous section, i.e. the Italian singers, although they were not yet outright Arcadian activists. This fledgling clique during its early days rallied around the Duchess of Shrewsbury who evidently had been affiliated with the Arcadians; her mother's first husband had served Queen Christina, the Arcadian patroness. [55] Originally from Italy, she converted to Protestantism and married the Duke of Shrewsbury in 1705. [56] Although members of the court regarded the Duchess unfavourably, she had considerable influence as a lady of the bedchamber to Queen Anne, and later to Caroline, the Princess of Wales. [57]

During the remainder of her life in England, she continued to participate in Italian interests and used her influence in this regard. For example, the Duchess was witness to an upheaval that consequently resulted with the triumph of the Italian singers at the Queen's Theatre in 1708–09. Evidently, the Duchess of Shrewsbury and the Duchess of Marlborough were present with other members of the nobility at a private recital featuring Nicolini and the English singer Mrs. Tofts in December 1708. Lady Wentworth recounted the following; Nicolini had conveyed his regrets and declined to perform, however the Duchess of Shrewsbury insisted on fetching him in her coach. Tofts then failed to perform as Nicolini had initially refused to attend and she departed in a rage; perhaps she viewed his refusal as a personal insult. White relates shortly after this episode, Tofts retired permanently from the stage in 1709, allowing the Italians to victoriously occupy the Queen's Theatre

---

[55] Ibid. p. 73.
[56] Ibid.
[57] Ibid. p. 74.

without further competition from English performers.[58] As we observe, the Duchess of Shrewsbury was biased towards the Italians, and therefore may be regarded as the first Arcadian activist in London.

An additional controversy, as formerly mentioned, concerns the Duke of Shrewsbury who allegedly conspired to ruin the English production of *Calypso and Telemachus*. According to the editor of John Huges' correspondence, a conspiratorial link between the Duke of Shrewsbury's actions and the Italian Duchess had been noted:

> Such was, at the time, the partiality in favour of Italian operas, that, after many such had been encouraged by large subscriptions, this of "Calypso and Telemachus", originally written and set in English after the Italian manner, was prepared with the usual expense of scenes and decorations; and being much crowded and applauded at the rehearsals, a subscription was obtained for it as usual. [i.e., raising the prices well above the general level]. This alarmed the whole Italian band, who apprehended that their harvest would soon be at an end, had interest enough, (the duke of Shrewsbury, whose dutches {sic} was an Italian, being Lord Chamberlain) to procure an order, the day before the performing of this opera, to take off the subscription for it, and to open the house at the lowest prices, or not at all. This was designed to sink it, but it failed of its end. It was however performed, tho' under so great Discouragement.[59]

---

[58] White, *English Opera*, pp. 148–150.

[59] John Huges, *Letters by Several Eminent Persons Deceased, Including the Correspondence of John Huges, Esq. (Author of The Siege of Damascus) and Several of His Friends* (London, 1773): I, in *Italian Circle*, p. 74. See also Knapp, 'A Forgotten Chapter.' Knapp's source; John Huges, ed. by William Duncombe, *Poems on Several Occasions*

Until her death in 1726, the Duchess remained one of the key figures associated with the Arcadian influenced Italian circle in London.[60] As time progressed, additional influential Italians arrived and strengthened this particular Italian clique and the Arcadian bond including the librettist Paolo Rolli, the castrato Francesco Bernardi ("Senesino") and Giovanni Bononcini the composer.[61] The Duchess was closely affiliated with Rolli in particular; for the present, we shall discuss his involvement with the Arcadians in London.

Rolli arrived in London in 1715 and was an influential addition to the Arcadian circle.[62] Apparently, Lord Stair invited him to England and they travelled together from Italy, whereby Rolli resided with Lord Stair for several months.[63] (Also, see Chapter 5.) As Dorris relates, having an Italian resident in the household was generally expected of the wealthy and intellectual echelons of society:

> The notion of an Italian resident in the household was not unusual in the London of the times. As Italian was considered one of the polite, hence ornamental languages, and as Italian music became increasingly fashionable, a domestic guide to these graces was considered desirable. For one who already spoke the language, a resident Italian provided the means of keeping in practise, and he would also serve to instruct those who had not yet learned the language. Further, the conversation of a man of learning can be edifying as well as delightful, and, finally, the pleasure of patronising the arts has always contained an element

(with some select essays in prose), (London: 1735), 2 Vols.
[60] Dorris, *Italian Circle*, p. 75.
[61] Ibid. p. 75.
[62] Ibid. p. 133.
[63] Ibid. pp. 133–136.

of prestige from being praised by the artist, which has always been an important part of patronage. Rolli was able to meet all of these conditions, including the frequent celebration of his patrons in dedications or poems, while his interest in science as well as in the fine arts seems to have made him from the beginning a familiar figure in the artistic and intellectual life of London, and hence an ornament to the noble household of a patron.[64]

Rolli's career in England included editing, writing, and teaching Italian to the Royal family and to the nobility;[65] as one would expect, Rolli concentrated his work on the Italian opera libretto. By observing the dedications of his works we obtain a record of his other patrons, which included Baron Dalrymple, and in particular, Lord Bathurst and the Earl of Burlington.[66]

Presently he became the focal point of the Arcadian-Italian circle for several reasons.[67] Rolli and Metastasio were both pupils of Gian-Vicenza Gravina who was one of the founding fathers of the Arcadian movement.[68] Rolli remained in contact with many prominent Arcadian-Italians while he resided in England; these individuals included, Antonio Conti, who introduced Shakespeare to

---

[64] Ibid. p. 136–137.

[65] Ibid. p. 10.

[66] Ibid. p. 139.

[67] In a poem written shortly after his arrival in London, "Capitole di Paolo Rolli romano, da Londra 1716," Rolli recorded the members of the circle he found there. The most important people mentioned are Antonio Conti, Riva, Nicolino, Bernachi, Marguerita de l'Épine, and Geminiani. Haym and Giacomo Rossi are also mentioned, but he must have perceived them as rivals and not a part of the group for he satirizes them in his Marziale in Albion epigrams. Dorris, Italian Circle, f. 33, p. 137.

[68] Ibid. pp. 11, 127.

the Italians, Antonio Cocchi, and the poet Scipione Maffei. In particular, he frequently corresponded with the Modenese diplomat Giuseppe Riva who was closely associated with Ludovico Muratori and Metastasio.[69] Essentially, Rolli was a direct link to those who embodied the ideals of the Arcadian movement, and effectively assumed the position as the unofficial leader of the Arcadian-influenced Italians in London; he was destined to play an active role in the tensions between the Italian circle[*] and Handel.

The Formation of the Opposing Factions

As we have observed, two opposing groups emerged before the Royal Academy was founded, and presently Handel would discover his position was situated between these factions, ultimately creating problems that would extend far into the future. Ironically, it stemmed from the introduction of Italian opera into England; the aim was to improve and advance English music, yet these intentions had been misconstrued. A major reason for this confusion, the previous attempts at translating Italian opera into English sounded ludicrous with the music to contemporary audiences; this also included bilingual operas with English and Italian texts. Ultimately this created a demand to hear authentic Italian opera in contrast to the polyglot that was produced.

As a result, two major factions surfaced at this date. The first factor concerned the Italian circle determined to eliminate the "nonsense" that was being produced in London. The second factor consisted of those who continued to promote their ambition of developing an English genre. Handel, due to his versatility in music,

---

[69] Ibid. pp. 10, 35.

[*] Hence, throughout the rest of this book, the term 'Italian circle' will refer to those influenced by Arcadian ideals and who were Rolli's supporters. Not all Italians in London were part of Rolli's clique, such as Nicola Haym and Rossi. (See f. 67).

interacted between these two factions as a catalyst for future problems. All three factions continually created friction; we shall now assess each group and the positions they assumed before the immediate foundation of the Royal Academy.

Rolli's Italian Circle: the Core and the Circumference

From its inception, two distinct groups within Rolli's circle were apparently operating a "working partnership" based on the terms of supply and demand. [70] At the core were the Italian-Arcadian activists, with their English patrons and promoters at the circumference — the Italians wished to impart their literature and culture to the English, and their patrons were eager to receive it. Where the production of Italian opera in London is concerned, the distinction between the two parts of this group is particularly important. While these two sections worked in harmony, Italian-Arcadian opera had the opportunity to flourish in London, however, when one or the other part of the group ceased to function in this fashion trouble was eminent, for instance, when the nobility patronised those who were considered to be outsiders, or on the fringes of the circle. The fact the English had their own ideals concerning opera production would also cause friction between these two parts of the circle.

Handel, although knowledgeable and well acquainted with Arcadian idealism, was willing to adapt to the English environment, and therefore was considered to be on the fringe of the group by those such as Rolli. As a result, a disturbance surfaced within the circle that would upset the balance; when the English began to selectively adopt the conventions that complied with their cultural preference, the Italians concluded their ideals were being

---

[70] While Dorris concentrates on the Italians in London and mentions those who patronised them, apparently he does not classify them into two different groups or sections. See *Italian Circle*, op. cit.

compromised.   Ultimately, these circumstances would cause dissensions later within the Royal Academy.

The English Genre Supporters

As already mentioned, the novelty of Italian opera had placed interest for English attempts aside, yet the issue was never fully abandoned; it had a brief window of opportunity to resurface when from 1717 onward new productions of opera ceased. This paucity in production resulted from unsecured financial support and the unstable court situation caused by the increasing problems between George I and the Prince of Wales. During this period, Handel experimented with English works under the patronage of the Earl of Carnarvon; he was a guest composer-in-residence at the Earl's home, and as such, he composed the two English masques *Acis and Galatea* and *Esther*.[71]   Notwithstanding Handel's eagerness to compose Italian opera according to English preferences, he was also agreeable when requested to compose other genres; this adaptable aspect of his character would be particularly important during his Covent Garden period when the Italian circle would eventually retaliate.

Handel as a Catalyst

Although Handel may not have intended to initiate any contentions, his versatility in composition seemed to have highlighted the fact, what the Italians had aspired to impart was not exactly what the English desired.

The difficulties concerning Italian opera in London corresponded with the English custom of assimilating foreign

---

[71] Christopher Hogwood, *Handel,* (New York: Thames and Hudson Inc., 1984. Reprint, 1995): pp. 72–74.

culture as a method of developing one's expertise in a particular subject. The Third Earl of Shaftsbury related the English were eager to learn from foreigners in order to acquire an appreciation of the arts from their original sources. The Earl noted his contemporaries believed by observing and/or copying masters from their place of origin, one achieves excellence in that area and thereby show all the refinements associated with "good-breeding":

> One who aspires to the character of a man of breeding and politeness is careful to form his judgement of arts and sciences upon right models of perfection. If he travels to Rome, he inquires which are the truest pieces of architecture, the best remains of statues, the best paintings of a Raphael or a Carraccio. However antiquated, rough, or dismal they may appear to him at first sight, he resolves to view them over and over, till he has brought himself to relish them, and finds their hidden graces and perfections ... Nor is he less careful to turn his ear from every sort of music besides that which is the best manner and truest harmony .... If a natural good taste be not already formed in us, why should not we endeavour to form it, and cultivate it till it become natural?[72]

Naturally, the Italians who were patronised by the nobility would be those whom one would refer to on matters related to Italian opera.

However, when Handel arrived in London in 1711, he inadvertently generated additional disturbances between the

---

[72] Third Earl of Shaftsbury's "Advice to an Author" in *Characteristics* quoted in H.A. Needham, ed., *Taste And Criticism in the Eighteenth Century*, (London: George Harrap, 1952): pp. 55–56, in Carole Taylor, Ph. D. Thesis, *Italian Operagoing in London, 1700–1745*, (Syracuse University: 1991), p. 131.

Arcadian Italians and their patrons. This may appear contradictory as it is accepted Handel was partial to Italian *opera seria* and contributed towards developing an appreciation for the genre in London when he returned from Germany in 1712. During this time, he composed several Italian operas that continued to whet the appetites of the English audiences; all the English opera revivals were in direct competition with his *Il Pastor Fido* in 1712, *Teseo* in 1713, and *Amadigi di Gaula* in 1715. One may speculate about the problems Handel initiated as the Italians encouraged the dissemination of their culture.

From the year 1711, Handel had played a major part in the anglicization of Italian opera with *Rinaldo* as we have previously observed. When *Rinaldo* was produced, Handel's opera was perceived as a prime example of the *Italian* style and his music was greatly admired, despite the fact Hill had intended this work to be accepted as an example of how the English could develop their own particular style. From this time onward, Handel was considered one of the most skilled composers of Italian opera available, and the fact the English held him in such high esteem, naturally, he would become the most sought after composer of Italian opera in London.

Additional elements that contributed to the appeal of *Rinaldo* were the machines and the spectacular scenery, which incidentally were anti-Arcadian. As we have observed from the section discussing the Arcadian movement, scenography was not considered important in Italy in contrast with the drama or text. The English, however, approved of these effects, and this would continue to be the norm in London; clearly, sets and costumes were considered an important component of an opera as we may observe from the various reports in the newspapers of the day. When a production featured new costumes and scenery this information was advertised to generate public interest, if a revival was produced with all original scenes and costumes it was announced in a similar fashion.[73] This would be one of the many differences opposing the Italian-Arcadian ideal with regard to Handel's operas.

Subsequent events suggest the Italians were not particularly pleased, and may have attempted to influence future decisions with respect to appropriate subjects. The Italians had previously interfered with the production of *Calypso and Telemachus* before Handel returned from Germany; Christopher Hogwood's description of Handel's *Il Pastor Fido* (1712) implies the choice of subject may have been influenced by the Italian presence in London:

> Handel's first venture of the operatic season was not well-judged. *Il Pastor Fido*, or *The Faithful Shepherd*, which was finished on 24 October and opened less than a month later, received a short shrift in an opera register (attributed to Francis Colman but undoubtedly by other hands, since it continues during the period he spent as a diplomat in Florence): 'The Scene represented only ye Country of Arcadia. ye Habits were old. — ye Opera Short'. The cast list shows that neither Nicolini nor Boschi was in England, which must have meant a major public disappointment; the music, written in Handel's deliberately simplified pastoral style, with none of the flamboyance of *Rinaldo*, a reduced number of arias (many of these both borrowed and monothematic) and very abbreviated recitative, represents an Italian ideal, less compelling and more stereotyped than English pastoral precedents

---

[73] For instance, the revival of Handel's *Amadigi* on June 20th, 1716 was announced in the *Daily Courant* as follows: "At the King's Theatre in the Hay-Market, this present Wednesday, being the 20th of June, will be perform'd an Opera call'd Amadis. With all the Scenes and Cloaths, belonging to this Opera : Particularly, the Fountain-Scene. To which will be added, Two New Symphonies." See Deutsch, p. 71.

of which Handel was probably ignorant.[74]

Judging from this description, *Il Pastor Fido* was a sweeping stylistic change when compared with *Rinaldo*; one can almost sense that Handel was probing the public's expectations. Interestingly, this description corresponds neatly with the ideals promoted by the Arcadian Crescimbeni whom we have mentioned previously; Handel had been patronised by the members of the Arcadian Academy while in Italy and was familiar with their ideals.[75] It is evident Handel was not averse to changing his style; this production may have been the delight of the Italians, yet the English were not impressed. Handel must have pondered upon their reaction and obviously decided to return to his flamboyant style of production with *Teseo* and *Amadigi di Gaula*.[76]

As we have just observed, the patrons' wishes and the goals of the Italians were varied; eminently, the simplified Arcadian ideal was not in favour. Handel had tested the pastoral convention, and discovered that a variation of the Italian style was required, incidentally, there is evidence that Handel approved of the English productions such as *Calypso and Telemachus*.[77] Handel willingly

---

[74] Hogwood, *Handel*, pp. 66–67.

[75] Ellen T. Harris, *Handel and the Pastoral Tradition* (London: Oxford University Press, 1980), pp. 56–57.

[76] Hogwood, *Handel*, pp. 67, 70.

[77] Knapp stated; "Perhaps the greatest compliment of all, which also comes in a roundabout way, is one quoted by Lowenberg. William Kitchener or Kitchiner ... wrote on the back of the ... 'Songs in ... Calypso and Telemachus', sold in Julian Marshall's sale, 29 July 1884, the following comment; 'Dr. Arnold told me Mr. Handell had so high an opinion of Calypso and Telemachus as to have declared he would have sooner have composed it than any one of his operas. W. K. 1813.' Since Arnold is said to have been known by Handel and advised him as a boy, the information is probably fairly reliable." From Knapp, 'A Forgotten Chapter,' p. 16. Knapp's sources; Alfred Lowenberg, *Annals of Opera*,

adapted his style of composition and apparently, he did not hold with the opinion that he was compromising his skills or artistry in the process. The nobility favoured Handel's eclectic compositions, and therefore they became divided in their preferences; while they wished to have Italian opera and follow the Italian model under the guidance of those they patronised, they also wanted it produced according to their requirements. Their selective preferences created many difficulties as the Italians were somewhat uncompromising in their ideals. A ripple in the Italian circle developed as the nobility at the circumference diverted their priorities from the accepted Italian/Arcadian traditions. The Italians at the core of the circle were dependant upon the nobility, and if the nobility were modifying their expectations and were "filtering" the ideals that the members of the core were presenting to them, the group as a whole could not continue to exist, or would at the very least, be placed in an uncompromising situation.

Although Handel may not have intentionally acted as a catalyst to these problems, he did not improve the situation as he assumed an active role in the production of his operas. Handel had personally supervised the production of *Rinaldo*, and Carole Taylor states this was "a first" in the establishment of Italian opera in England, i.e. that the composer should monitor a production.[78] Therefore, under these circumstances, Handel had achieved a unique position, and this may have provided an additional source of aggravation for the Italians. As previously discussed, the composer was considered one of the least important contributors regarding the creation of an opera in Italy.

Consequently, a polemical struggle generated by this situation would continue to cause upheaval. Apart from the problems occurring within the two sections of the Italian circle, the

---

2nd ed. (Geneva: 1955): p. 117 and *Dictionary of National Biography*, (London: 1885): ii, p. 111.

[78] See her thesis, *Italian Operagoing in London*, p. 29.

English-genre supporters would prove a further irritation for the Italians in the future. Perhaps the most decisive factor was the Italians' disapproval of Handel's willingness to compose in a manner that conformed with English tastes and customs, and more importantly, that he as a composer should have been granted this prodigious level of authority with the production of opera. Obviously, the Italians could not properly introduce their ideals of reformed Italian opera to the unique underdeveloped operatic territory of London as they existed in Italy if the English preferences were catered to. The same applies when the composer has been allocated more control; it may have been viewed that the music, as a result of his involvement, would encroach upon the realm of the drama, which was not the Arcadian aim. When the Royal Academy was founded, a battlefield was also established where these unresolved tensions were to be vented.

Chapter 2

The Royal Academy of Music,
or the "Royal Anarchy of Music"?

Now that we have established the formation of the various factions, so diverse in their ideology, that comprised the opera circle of London, in this chapter we will explore how they affected the foundation and management of the Royal Academy. First, we will examine the different viewpoints of the various groups and what they had possibly aspired to achieve within the company; perhaps each group perceived individual opportunities and entertained ambitious expectations concerning this venture that may have clashed. Subsequently we may discover how these various ideologies may have initiated the problems that culminated in its untimely demise.

The English Patrons of the Italian Circle
and the Assimilation Issue

If we view the first collapse of Italian opera in England (1717–19) from a positive perspective, we may deduce this resulted with a beneficial outcome; the nobility realised from their experience that although a following for Italian opera had been established, a financially stable company was required to prevent a repetition of this failure. By 1719, plans for this newly proposed opera company were in the formative stage, and judging from the sequence of events, it is evident that the English were primarily interested in a venture that corresponded with their cultural aesthetics.

The nobility and impresarios were concentrating on the musical aspect of opera contrary to Arcadian ideology. Despite the consensus that librettos in England, as in Italy, were regarded as the most unacceptable form of literature,[79] there was no emphasis on the reformation of the libretto as a literary genre in England. The English had a thriving theatrical and literary culture and did not consider it necessary to transform another genre, in contrast to the situation experienced by the Arcadians in Italy who failed to establish a national theatrical style and attempted to assimilate opera to accommodate their own designs. As a result, opera was accepted by the English as a separate theatrical genre due to its musical aspect, and therefore they considered music the most important component. When we study the procedures that established the Royal Academy this cultural difference becomes apparent.

In January 1719, a petition was presented to the King requesting patents for this venture. According to a letter written by the Lord Chamberlain to Attorney General Lechmemer, "Several Gentlemen who desire to be incorporated by Letters patents for the *Encouragement of Music*" presented this petition.[80] In addition, the title "The Royal Academy of Music" illustrates the English perception of opera as primarily a unique *musical* genre.

The founding members of the company had already decided that Handel should be composer for the Royal Academy; Mainwaring stated they requested Italian operas composed by Handel:

---

[79] According to Smith, this perception in England concerning librettos originated from the time John Dryden had written his condemnation of them in his preface to *Albion and Albanius* (1685). See Ruth Smith, *Handel's Oratorios and Eighteenth-Century Thought*, (Cambridge University Press: 1995), pp. 30, and f. 84, p. 369.

[80] Judith Milhous and Robert D. Hume, 'New Light on Handel and The Royal Academy of Music in 1720,' *Theatre Journal*, XXV (1983): p. 150. My italics.

> The intention of this musical Society, was to secure to themselves a constant supply of Operas to be composed by Handel, and performed under his direction. For this end a subscription was set on foot: {...}[81]

Strikingly, Handel was granted unprecedented control with regard to the musical sector of the Academy; not only was he designated the director of the orchestra, Mainwaring's comment also dares to suggest Handel was a significant factor concerning the foundation of the Academy in the first instance. True, Mainwaring may have been biased towards Handel to the point of exaggerating his importance within the Academy, but it cannot be disproved that Handel was a primary consideration with the formative plans and was to assume a prominent role in the company.

In May 1719, Handel received instructions from the Duke of Newcastle, perhaps a requisite of his duties, to engage the finest singers he could procure in Italy and Germany.[82] This assignment was unconventional when we consider the surviving minutes from a meeting held by the directors dated November 27th, 1719. The treasurer and his deputy were not yet appointed, and the day-to-day managerial policies of the Academy had not been determined such as Heidegger's expense projections and the "Court Days" for the directors:

27 November 1719

At a Court of Directors of the Royal Academy of Musick

---

[81] Mainwaring, p. 97.

[82] Milhouse and Hume, 'New Light,' pp.150–151. The Duke was Lord Chamberlain at the time, and as Lord Chamberlain he was the governor of the Academy.

Present: Governour, Deputy Governour; Directors: Duke of Montague, Duke of Portland, Lord Bingley, Mr Bruce, Mr Mildmay, Mr Fairfax, Mr Blathwayte, Mr Harrison, Mr Smith, Mr Whitworth, Doctor Arbuthnot, Mr Heidegger.

Ordered —

That a Letter be writ to Mr Hendell to make an Offer to Durastante of Five hundred pounds Sterling for three months to commence from the first day of March next or sooner if possible, And that in Case she continues here the remainder of fifteen months, Eleven hundred pounds more, if not, One hundred pounds to bear her expenses home.

That Mr Hendell be Ordered to return to England & bring with him Grunswald the Bass upon the terms he proposes. And that he bring with him the proposalls of all the Singers he has treated with, particularly Cajetano Orsini.

That Doctor Arbuthnot be desired to treat with Mrs Robinson.

That Mr Heidegger be desir'd to speak to Galeratti and Beneditti to send their proposals to commence the First Day of March next.

That a Treasurer be declared.

That his Deputy shall give Security and have a Sallary.

That the Honourable James Bruce Esqr. be Treasurer.

That there be a Call of Five per Cent of the Subscribers on or before 19th Day of December next.

That Mr Heidegger be desir'd to lay before the Directors on Monday next [November 30, 1719] an Estimate of the Charges of the Opera house, and of the Officers that are necessary to manage the Same.

51

That Mondays Wensdays & Fridays be Court
Days for the Directors.
Adjourn'd to Monday next.[83]

It is obvious that the engagement of the singers received
precedence over the organization of the Academy's foundation and
management policies; perhaps this is a further indication that the
musical element of opera was more important in England.

These two situations, i.e. the music orientated nature of the
Academy's establishment and the fact a composer would be allocated
this distinctive authority, may have proved to be the two main
causes of friction encountered by Handel. As we have observed, this
situation was anti-Arcadian and may have initiated a power play
between Handel and Rolli's Italians concerning who would
eventually obtain the support of the directors.

Manifestation of the Problems

Rolli, in his surviving letters, manifests the initial signs of
discord occurring within the Royal Academy, and it is apparent he
was not amiable towards Handel from the beginning:

Paolo Antonio Rolli to Abbate Giuseppe Riva
(Translated)

Thistleworth, 13 July, 1719.

{...} The Man [Handel?] loves and hides his feelings;
but *quousque*

---

[83] Ibid. pp. 151–152.

tandem? {...}[84]

The next clue suggesting Rolli may have generated further aggravation for Handel is obvious in his complaint regarding the singers who have been selected:

Rolli to Riva (Translated)

Richmond, I don't know which day of August 1719.

{...} It is said for certain that Durastanti will be coming for the Operas: Oh! what a bad choice for England! I shall not enter into her singing merits but she really is an Elephant! They are still saying that Borosini is the tenor coming and not Guicciardi! {...}[85]

Unfortunately the first letter fails to explain Rolli's animosity towards Handel, however, the second letter begins to shed some light; Handel had been granted the authority on May 14th, 1719 to choose the singers he considered most suitable for the venture:

Instructions to Mr Hendel.

That Mr. Hendel either by himself or such correspondence as he shall think fit to procure proper Voices to Sing in the Opera. {...} Holles Newcastle.[86]

---

[84] Deutsch, p. 92. 'The Man' must represent Handel. Rolli often refers to him in this manner, and has assigned Handel other sarcastic titles in his various letters. For instance, in a letter dated January 25th, 1729 he calls Handel "Alto" [the Great Man.] See Deutsch, pp. 249–250.

[85] Deutsch, p. 94.

[86] Ibid. p. 90.

Noticeably, the directors did not mention Durastanti until 27th November 1719; six months after Handel had been issued these directives:

From the Minutes of the Royal Academy of Music,

27 November 1719

{...}

Ordered;
    That a Letter be writ to Mr Hendell to make an Offer to Durastante of Five hundred pounds Sterling for three months to commence from the first day of March next or Sooner if possible, {...}[87]

It is possible Handel had suggested Durastanti first; she had performed in his earlier opera *Agrippina* that had been produced in Venice December 1709 while he was in Italy, and therefore he would have been well acquainted with her artistic capabilities.[88] Handel may have informed the directors that she was presently in Dresden and advised them she was an acceptable choice. The singer was not mentioned by the directors in surviving sources before Handel's visit to Dresden where he engaged her, and they finally refer to her when a considerable period had elapsed between the time of Handel's instructions of May and his next orders originating from November. Therefore, it is evident Handel had time to inform the directors by correspondence stating she was suitable for engagement and they agreed with his decision.

---

[87] Ibid. p. 96.
[88] Ibid. p. 27.

Why should this cause friction with Rolli? There is one possible explanation. We have observed previously in the section discussing the Arcadian Academy that the composer was not usually allocated great authority with the production of opera, which also included his own works. Rolli may have been particularly annoyed that Handel was granted this signal privilege; compounding this problem, Handel was influencing the directors to choose singers, who in Rolli's opinion, were not acceptable.

We have also noted the singers according to Italian tradition were exceptionally important as they were the reciters of the poetic text of the *dramma per musica*, and therefore the singers' role in presenting the drama was crucial where the Italian librettists were concerned. *Opera seria* was extremely vital to Italian dramatists as it was virtually the only dramatic genre available in Italy. If Rolli was interested in disseminating the ideals associated with Italian drama, he may have decided that his choice of singers was more appropriate. It is also noteworthy that he corresponded his complaints to another member of the "Inner" Italian circle of London — the Modenese diplomat Riva — and complained Durastanti was "a bad choice for England." Apparently, Rolli was reporting to members of the "inner-sanctum" on how unreceptive the English were to Italian ideals. He did not approve of Durastanti for England, for perhaps he concluded she was incapable of presenting the Italian ideal and would impede the introduction of their culture, or may convey an incorrect first impression.

Could it be possible Rolli was preoccupied with imparting the correct impression of Italian culture to the English? The explanation that he may have viewed her as an obstacle to the presentation of his own librettos is a strong motive. In the wake of the precarious introduction of Italian opera to England, Rolli may have considered the Royal Academy as the perfect opportunity to demonstrate how opera ought to be produced. He may have deduced that Durastanti would impede his aim within the Royal Academy, which was probably perceived by him and the members of the "Inner" Italian circle as the ideal medium of introducing Italian culture "correctly". The fact Rolli was disgruntled they had not considered his choice of "superior" performers supports this explanation.

An additional indication of discord within the Royal Academy was displayed when Rolli's Italian circle increased with the arrival of the castrato Senesino followed by the composer Bononcini; again, we have Rolli's letters relating the next series of events:

Rolli to Riva (Translated)

London, 29th August 1720.

{…} No news yet from Bononcini. {…}[89]

Rolli to Riva (Translated)

London, 23rd September 1720.

On Monday last Senesino arrived in company with Berselli and Salvi. I heard the news while dining in Richmond on Tuesday and at once came up to town with our dear Casimiro. I am delighted to find this famous artist a man well-mannered, well-read, extremely kind and endowed with noblest sentiments. Dear Riva, if it is ever true that one recognises a fine day from a fine morning, believe me it is the great exception to the rule. {…}

The Alpine Proteus [Handel] has spoken of me in terms of great esteem to Casimiro, who has proved clearly to him on several occasions that I deserve some

---

[89] Ibid. p. 111.

consideration. Dear Riva, I submit myself to all shows of humility towards him within the limits of decorum, and we shall see whether that bristly nature of his will soften. Yesterday I was called by the Board of the Royal Academy and commissioned to examine and shorten *Il Dramma dell' Amore e Maestà* (The Drama of Love and Majesty). I should make no progress without our Senesino and both of us would be at a loss without Haydeger; now you see if we can do no more! How I rejoice that Senesino has such a clever mind and understands the Cabel to perfection! We are expecting you to come and make up the Triumvirate. {...}[90]

The first excerpt illustrates Rolli eagerly awaited the arrival of Bononcini, while the second letter reveals further information and elaborates upon his strained relationship with Handel. Apparently, at this point Handel voiced no animosity towards Rolli as he acknowledged him with "great esteem" to Casimiro; yet, we observe an interesting detail, Casimiro had approached Handel on Rolli's behalf and requested he receive more consideration. Handel did not display any particular preference for Rolli's texts during the course of the Royal Academy and set more librettos by Nicola Haym than those of Rolli, as we shall explore later. It would appear that Handel had established preferences for his work policies at an early date, and this may explain Rolli's antagonism and condescending tone concerning Handel's inflexibility.

With regard to the second excerpt, we notice Rolli hesitated to comply with the instructions assigned to him to shorten the opera *Amore e Maestà* without Senesino or Heidegger's opinions.[91] Rolli apparently did not wish to attempt any changes without the advice of the principal singer; as stated, the principal singers had

---

[90] Ibid. pp. 112–113.

[91] Apparently, the directors had the opportunity to meet Senesino first before Rolli was able to meet with him as the following excerpts show.

considerable authority according to the Arcadian tradition in Italy, and apparently, Rolli advocated this convention. In addition, it seems Heidegger was acting as a spokesperson for Rolli, so perhaps Rolli was having difficulties with the directors concerning the production of the opera and required Heidegger's influential assistance.

Accordingly, Rolli affirms that Senesino understood the prevailing atmosphere and the "machinations" of the Academy; Rolli describes the Academy as a "cabal", suggesting he suspected or was attentive to arcane collusions occurring behind the scenes. Interestingly, this cabal-reference immediately follows his account of the request issued by the directors to shorten the opera; he may have viewed this assignment as an effort to thwart "authentic" productions of Italian opera. He may also have suspected an "intrigue" opposing him and his Italian-Arcadian comrades; notice how Rolli expected Riva to complete the "Triumvirate."[92] Rolli appears to have sarcastically perceived the directors as the "Senate" that must be protected from all external influences, suggesting he was displeased with the eclectic nature of the Royal Academy. If Rolli viewed the Academy from this perspective, it is obvious he was objecting to the management of the venture at this point; as a result, a rift between the "Inner-core" and the circumference of the Italian circle had manifested itself. The following two letters will elaborate on our observations of the previous correspondence:

Rolli to Riva (Translated)

London, 29th September 1720.

{...} I am waiting anxiously for Senesino, whom

---

[92] This term refers to the political alliance made between Pompey the Great, Julius Caesar, and Marcus Crassus in 60BC. This alliance was designed to carry out plans of political aggrandisement against the opposition to the Roman Senate.

I shall try to ingratiate with every art known to me and I shall explain everything to him in all honesty.

No other news from Bononcini, since I heard that he had received the money sent to him {...}[93]

Rolli to Riva (Translated)

London, 18th October 1720.

You must know that Madame Salvai has brought Polani* with her from Holland; {...} I must tell you that Margherita, in conjunction with our Senesino, proposed the opera of "Amore e Maestà". Which opera cannot be performed as at Florence, because it would then have so much endless recitative and so few arias, that Senesino would have only four in all, I was therefore instructed to polish it up and in accord with them both I removed and added and changed as was necessary. The Alpine Faun [Handel] according to the ancient system which he always proposes, in order to show that what has been done is the same as it was before, proposed Polani to rearrange and direct the opera. Our Senesino, naturally enough was furious: the opera had been proposed by him, new music was necessary for the additional part and for that he wanted it to be varied; he was opposed to making a pastiche of old arias and wanted to have a man at the harpsichord; at his first outburst he [Handel] called him a damned Fool; these were all the motives for his resentment.

---

[93] Deutsch, p. 113–114.

* "Polani was a Venetian singer and composer, recently arrived in England. Nothing, however, is known of his connection with the Haymarket Opera." Deutsch, p. 115.

The Faun obliged me to tell him not to oppose him and I was the bearer of the Faun's embassy. But I could not restrain him [Senesino] and I advised him to go himself to speak to him [Handel] with gentle firmness and say to him that he wished to show all due deference to his advice, but that as regarded his personal estimation he begged him to take into consideration all the above-mentioned arguments; that he entertained no personal animosity against anyone except Polani, but that he would have sung under him in any other opera which the Directors themselves might wish to choose; not however, an opera which he himself had proposed and for the success of which the Board of Directors had made him responsible; in short that it not being possible to perform this opera as it then was, there was no occasion for performing it in such a manner; that he did not propose anyone else, while the Academy had at its disposal excellent musicians. The Man [Handel] was taken aback and asked him if this was a trick of mine ... [unreadable word], but he obtained a non-committal reply and was informed that I had already given a copy of the opera to Polani and had only explained to him the Board's opinions so as to guide Polani, adding furthermore that he had not come to direct operas but to be a musician. Believe me, he [Senesino] spoke with remarkable eloquence, if he worded the reply as he repeated it to me. Rest assured also that the very first opera would fail utterly if directed by that stupid man — and all to the delight of the Savage [Handel]. Tomorrow Senesino must go before the Board of Directors; he is this evening at Richmond at the repeated request of the Royal Prince [of Wales] who is quite carried away by him, {...} Those Directors, who have already come to know of the facts, such as Arbuthnot and the most estimable Blaithwaite, have declared that they will be at the Board tomorrow of set purpose to do all that Signor Senesino shall desire because he is in the right; and as the whole affair is proceeding with utmost smoothness and restraint, so we hope the Man [Handel] will set a good face on a bad game. But I am amused that he should suspect me and not trust my most polite manners in his majestic and Faunlike presence. {...}

Bononcino {Bononcini} is here already. {...} I am gradually instructing him and telling him the remuneration [due to me]. I find him well disposed to do his duty and my principal advice to him is to keep himself united to Senesino. He has already conceived a high opinion of him because he is very able. [94]

The letter dated September 23rd implies that Rolli did not want to waste any time in becoming acquainted with Senesino who was capable of recognising the bureaucracy of the "Cabal," and therefore would be a welcome addition and reinforce the core of the Italian-Arcadian clique. An intriguing question; what exactly did Rolli want to "explain" to Senesino as stated in the letter dated September 29th? The term "explain everything" could also imply an attempt to disclose the morale-atmosphere prevailing apart from the day-to-day issues of schedules, practise sessions, etc. It is also interesting that in the second letter dated October 18th, Rolli advises Bononcini to keep "himself united" to Senesino. Obviously, Rolli was campaigning for support from sympathetic Italians and confirming their allegiance.

The letter from October is of particular interest to us as Rolli relates the events that mark the beginning of the tensions between Senesino and Handel, including the aggravation of existing problems. Evidently, Handel refused to set an opera suggested by

---

[94] Ibid. pp. 114–115.

Senesino, and voiced no objection to another composer accomplishing this task. Handel's decision to allow Polani compile a pasticcio is rather confusing and almost contradictory regarding the conflicts surrounding the ideals of the Arcadian-influenced Italians; apparently, Handel approved of "the ancient system" regarding pasticcios, so at least in this area he was not contrary to Arcadian practise.

Handel was very defensive with regard to his position of authority within the Academy, and this became evident with the skirmish involving *Amore e Maestà*. Senesino's request does not seem exorbitant, (in fact, it is quite flattering).[95] However, Handel may have been indignant that his decision was challenged by a person not privileged to his thoughts on this subject and therefore whom he believed had no right to question his actions; this may explain why he called Senesino a "fool". Handel may not have been familiar with Senesino's capabilities and perhaps decided to wait before he composed for him; this may be one possible reason why Handel would suggest another composer work on that proposed opera. Winton Dean and John Merrill Knapp stated each text had to be altered specifically for the singers of a cast; the composer and the poet had to consider the size of the cast, and also each singer's voice pitch and their technical ability before they could commence their work.[96]

---

[95] Handel apparently was disgusted with attempts made by others to flatter him, and this may have fostered his feelings of mistrust. Charles Jennens wrote this anecdote in his copy of Mainwaring's biography of Handel; "{…} Handel told me that the words of Il Trionfo &c. were written by Cardinal Pamphilli, & added 'an old Fool!' I ask'd 'why Fool? because he wrote an Oratorio? perhaps you will call *me* fool for the same reason!' He answer'd 'So I would, if you flatter'd me, as He did'." See Winton Dean's article 'Charles Jennen's Marginalia to Mainwaring's Life of Handel,' *Music and Letters* Vol. 53, No. 2 (April, 1972): p. 166.

[96] Winton Dean and John Merrill Knapp, *Handel's Operas; 1704–1726* (Oxford: Clarendon Press, 1987), p. 16.

An additional possibility — the drama may not have captured his imagination, and this may have influenced Handel's decision not to work on that particular opera. Dean commented that Handel was more creative with a libretto that attracted his attention:

> But when Handel could identify himself with the plot, and especially when the librettist laid it out in a manner combining human sympathy with dramatic conviction, his imagination was strong enough to reconcile the contrary forces of artistic unity and a centrifugal convention, and (by harnessing the friction between them) to bring off effects unattainable in any other medium [i.e. opera seria]. [97]

While Handel's convictions concerning that particular opera have not been established, apparently he was not impressed as Amadei set it later for Senesino under the title *Arsace*, February 1st, 1721.[98]

Ironically, Handel may have been acting for the mutual benefit of all involved, while Senesino was just plain stubborn. The fact Handel would not capitulate marks the beginning of a tug-of-war struggle concerning who would maintain control: the composer, or the singer. This argument then continued and permeated the atmosphere of the Academy, also influencing their admirers; at this date we observe Arbuthnot and Blaithwaite supporting Senesino in this instance, indicating ominous forebodings for the future. Handel suspects Rolli of foul play, emphasising the seriousness of this situation.

Tensions continued to develop as the rivalry between the various composers of the Academy escalated. An intriguing question, how did this rivalry develop when Handel was obviously

---

[97] Winton Dean, *Handel and the Opera Seria* (United States: University of California Press Ltd., 1969), p. 22.
[98] Deutsch, p. 122.

willing to allow another composer, i.e. Polani, arrange and direct an opera? In addition, Porta's *Numitore* had opened the first season of the Academy, April 2nd, 1720, and Handel must have been aware that other composers were expected to take part.[99] Handel was master of the orchestra; therefore, it is logical to assume that he was informed regarding who would participate in the proceedings of the Academy. If we resume with Mainwaring's account, we may discover additional information regarding this situation, however his book is frustrating in certain areas as he apparently relied on information based on anecdotes and in the process confused several of the facts.[100] For instance, he states that the *first* problems exhibited at the Academy were instigated by Bononcini and Amadei who were in competition with Handel:

> At this time BUONONCINI and ATTILIO composed for the Opera, and had a strong party in their favour. Great reaction they saw to be jealous of such a rival as HANDEL, and all the interest they had was employed to decry his Music, and hinder him from coming to the Haymarket; but these attempts were defeated by the powerful avocation above-mentioned, at whose desire he had just been to Dresden for Singers.[101]

Subsequently, Mainwaring relates the problems with Senesino. However, according to the letters by Rolli quoted previously, we are aware Bononcini had not yet composed for the Academy before Handel was experiencing trouble with Senesino. In addition, Amadei's first opera for the Academy would be performed

---

[99] Bononcini and Giovanni Porta for instance. See the article 'New Light' by Milhous and Hume, pp. 152–153.

[100] According to the new forward by J. Merrill Knapp, Mainwaring apparently relied on information from John Christopher Smith Jr. See Mainwaring, p. VI.

[101] Mainwaring, p. 98.

later.[102]   Therefore, we may conclude that the first incidents of discord were the problems Handel encountered with Rolli and Senesino, and not Bononcini and Amadei as Mainwaring states.

Compounding this confusion, Mainwaring moulds into one occasion the time of the premiere and the first revision of Handel's *Radamisto* of 1720.   If we can determine which performance he is referring to, the exact cause of the tensions between Handel and the other composers may be disclosed.   Directly after the above-mentioned quote, Mainwaring continues:

> In the year 1720, he [Handel] obtained leave to perform his Opera of RADAMISTO. If persons who are now living, and who were present at that performance may be credited, the applause it received was almost as extravagant as his AGRIPPINA had excited: the crowds and tumults of the house at Venice were hardly equal to those at LONDON. {...}
>
> But, it may be thought, that the great excellence of SENESINO, both as to voice and action, might have a considerable share in the wonderful impressions made upon the audience. For, by virtue of great advantages in the representation, many performances of little or no value, have not only passed, but been well received — To the ladies especially, the merits of SENESINO would be much more obvious, than those of HANDEL. — Perhaps they would. That all depended on the Composer, I am as far from asserting, as I am from believing that any other person could have shewn such a singer to equal advantage. Let any impartial and competent judge consider, whether it is likely that the whole musical world could have afforded a composer besides himself, capable of furnishing SENESINO with

---

[102] This opera was *Arsace*, February 1st, 1721.
Deutsch, p. 122.

such a song, as that of Ombra Cara in the very Opera before us.[103]

The fact Mainwaring mentions the public's reception of Senesino's performance in *Radamisto* obviously implies that he is referring to the *revised production* of December 28th, 1720, which was Senesino's first opera composed by Handel for the Academy. Strikingly, Mainwaring opens a debate concerning who could present Senesino's capabilities more proficiently than Handel. Reviewing the information presented concerning the controversy surrounding *Amore e Maestà*, the situation is clarified.

Senesino had requested to have the finest composer available to set the work in question and at this early date a group supported Senesino in his decision upon Handel completing this task. However, the project apparently was delayed due to the controversy concerning Polani and was subsequently postponed until Amadei set it later with the title *Arsace*. In the interim, Bononcini produced his opera for Senesino, *Astarto*, on November 19th, 1720 before Handel revised *Radamisto* for December. If we continue where we adjourned with Mainwaring's account, it is evident that the rivalry between the followers of the composers commenced when Handel excelled with his revision for Senesino:

> The great success of it {i.e. Handel's revision of *Radamisto* for Senesino} matur'd the project before concerted for establishing the academy. For it could not be effected at once, as a considerable number of great persons had been influential in bringing over BUONONCINI and ATTILIO. And these foreigners they were the more unwilling to abandon, because they really had abilities in their professions. Perhaps the contest ran high on both sides, as if the object of them

---

[103] Mainwaring, pp. 98–101.

had been much more important. Yet I cannot agree with some, who think then of no importance, and treat them as ridiculous. Those who thought their humour engaged to support the old Composers; who really preferred them to HANDEL; or fancied that it was a defect of humanity, or an act of injustice to discard them, not because they were unfit for their office, but because another foreigner was come, who was thought to be fitter; — had surly a right to interest themselves warmly in their defence, at a time when they were so much in want of assistance.

And those, on the other hand, might as reasonably join in opposing them, who were firmly convinced of HANDEL's great superiority; and who though it for the honour of the nation to enlist in its service the most eminent artists. The old ones, in their opinion, had no right to complain of any preference given to another, provided they were duly paid for the time they had been engaged. {...}[104]

Notwithstanding that the musical capabilities of the various composers were contrasted, obviously, the composer who could present Senesino with the finest operas also became a factor in the equation. Perhaps if Handel had been more obliging when first requested to set *Amore e Maestà* this particular incident might have been settled directly; as a result, Senesino may not have become argumentative, and the presence of the other composers may not have proved "threatening" for Handel. However, Handel was adamant in defending his convictions, and therefore may have inadvertently fuelled the rivalry between the composers. He did not object if other composers were introduced to the Academy, providing they did not pose a threat to his position; but Senesino's

---

[104] Ibid. pp. 101–103.

admirers expected him to be presented with operas by the most capable composer. This may account for the introduction of *Muzio Scevola* as the deciding factor concerning the composers' capabilities, for Handel, Bononcini, and Amadei were each commissioned to compose one act. Here we will resume with Mainwaring's comments:

> Such then was the state of things in the year 1720, at the time RADAMISTO was performed. The succeeding winter brought this musical disorder to its crisis. In order to terminate all matters in controversy, it was agreed to put them on this fair issue. The several parties concerned were to be jointly employed in making an Opera, in which each of them was to take a different act. And he, who by the general suffrage, should be allowed to have given the best proofs of his abilities, was to be put into possession of the house. The proposal was accepted, whether from choice or necessity, I cannot say. The event was answerable to the expectations of HANDEL'S friends. His act was the last, and the superiority of it very manifest, that there was not the least pretense for any further doubts or disputes. {...} The name of the Opera was MUZIO SCÆVOLA.
>
> The academy being now firmly established, and HANDEL appointed Composer to it, all things went on prosperously for a course of between nine and ten years.[105]

Apparently, as a result of this controversy, Handel's career at the Academy ultimately rested upon the outcome of this contest. The first problem Handel experienced with Senesino concerning

---

[105] Ibid. pp. 104–106.

Amore e Maestà had sparked a side effect that may have endangered Handel's position within the Academy, and this may explain why the rivalry became more problematic. Let us return to Mainwaring's account; "The great success of it {i.e. Handel's revision of *Radamisto* for Senesino} matur'd the project before concerted for establishing the academy." He implies not all matters concerning the management and organisation of the Royal Academy were finalized, including who would be selected as head composer; it appears they deferred this decision due to the fact the other composers were also requested to participate in the company. This development is evident in the surviving minutes dated November 30th, 1719 relating the foundation of the Academy. Handel had been designated master of the orchestra, however following this statement, Bononcini was also requested to compose music and conduct the orchestra:

30 November, 1719

At a court of Directors of the Royal Academy of Musick

{...} that Mr Hendell be Master of the Orchester with a Sallary.

It is also the opinion of the Directors That Segnr Bona Cini be writ to, To know his Terms for composing & performing in the Orchester. [sic.] [106]

This implied that Bononcini would assume control of the orchestra for specific occasions; obviously, Handel viewed his position within the Academy was threatened by Bononcini as he was proposed and accepted by the directors first. This may have exasperated the situation, particularly when Rolli, whom he

---

[106] Milhous and Hume, 'New Light,' p. 152.

distrusted, was attempting to unite the Italians in an intimidating manner.

In review, the initial conflicts within the Academy apparently stemmed from the "rebellion" by the Italians in opposition to the directors and the authority delegated to Handel in an anti-Arcadian fashion. Rolli was displeased with Handel's particular involvement and the decisions he reached regarding the employment of the first company of singers. The directors and the eclectic style of opera they produced also irritated him, for he rallied sympathetic Italians and patrons for support. We now observe a division within Rolli's Italian circle in London between the Italian "Inner-core" and their English supporters at the circumference. The fact Handel would not capitulate to Senesino's wishes, perhaps due to personal artistic motives, aggravated the whole situation; this ignited a heated controversy concerning who should compose operas for Senesino, and as a result, who was qualified for the position of House Composer. Handel was finally deemed the composer *par excellence*, however, this consensus failed to end the rivalries; the factions that had been created would disrupt future proceedings in the Royal Academy.

The Problems Escalate

From the time of the Royal Academy's foundation, Handel was establishing and defending his position within that institution, and continued to do so. The new conflicts emerging would be related to Handel's insistence on remaining involved with his compositions, and the right to control other aspects of his opera productions; one issue in particular — the setting of librettos.

Rolli's contempt for Handel apparently had roots planted deeply in the issue of text setting. Earlier, we noted that Handel was not inclined to collaborate with Rolli, and this in part stems from his quest for control over his operas. Handel did not work as a mere "text–setter" of music as he was actively involved with the alterations to the librettos of his various operas. As previously mentioned, Handel was interested in a libretto that inspired his creativity, and Rolli's texts apparently did not measure up to his expectations. Dean and Knapp state:

> In those he prepared for Handel {i.e. the librettos} he never failed to muddle the development of the plot and the motivation of the characters, with the result that every product of their collaboration is seriously flawed.[107]

Alternatively, Handel preferred to collaborate with Nicola Haym who apparently possessed a congenial nature; obviously, Handel could influence Haym with more success than Rolli. Dean and Knapp state the following concerning Haym and his collaboration with Handel:

> Haym, {...} was a man of a very different calibre. A cellist, composer, book-collector, and antiquarian rather than a man of letters {...}. He played a significant part in establishing opera in London. For several possible reasons — because he was himself a musician, or took a more modest attitude to his duties, or proved temperamentally more compatible — Haym's collaboration with Handel was infinitely more fruitful than Rolli's. All the masterpieces of the Royal Academy years are based on Haym's librettos, or rather his skilful adaptation of the work of others. While his abridgement of the recitative (except *Tamerlano*) was severe and occasionally cut the corner of the plot too fine, unlike Rolli he retained many aria texts, and so preserved much of the quality of his sources. Since

---

[107] Dean and Knapp, *Handel's Operas*, p. 17.

Salvi, Piovene, and others were competent practitioners, Handel generally received from Haym a workmanlike text with a coherent plot and consistent characters.[108]

Reviewing the list of productions for the Royal Academy, we may note the collaborative process in the production of each new opera. (See Appendix Two.) There are fifteen new operas in total; almost half of the new productions were composed by Handel, including the pasticcios and *Muzio Scevola*. Nine of the new productions were composed by Bononcini including *Muzio Scevola*. Eight (including works marked '?') were by Ariosti, and two by Amadei including *Muzio Scevola*. One opera remaining is *Narciso* by Scarlatti. This totals thirty-five new productions; on further analysis:

• Handel had five operas with texts by Rolli, (six if the work marked '?' is taken into account) — amounting to only one third of his output. The remainder, eight (or ten counting the '?'- operas) were by Haym.
• Bononcini had six librettos by Rolli, two by Haym, and one possibly arranged by himself. Rolli's texts therefore amount to two-thirds of Bononcini's output, outnumbering those he wrote for Handel.
• Both of Amadei's works have text by Rolli.
• Ariosti had *no* librettos by Rolli. All of Ariosti's texts were by Haym, including two that were possibly written by Haym specifically.[109]

Obviously, Haym's librettos dominated the Royal Academy;

---

[108] Ibid.
[109] Interestingly, Dean and Knapp surmise Haym's librettos for Ariosti were less effective because Ariosti may not have exercised as much control over his productions, as Handel was accustomed to wield. Ibid. f. 15, p. 17.

he contributed to fourteen operas — twenty if the question-marked operas are considered. Rolli contributed to thirteen of all the new productions; fourteen if we consider the question-marked opera. Handel's interest in remaining involved with the text alterations may have been the primary reason he chose Haym, and may account for the success they achieved with these operas in comparison with those Rolli contributed to. Apparently, Handel encountered less difficulty with Haym when extensively altering the texts according to Dean and Knapp:

> What we should like to know of course is the extent to which Handel was personally responsible for the London alterations. We do have some pointers. There are several instances, for example, *Radamisto* and *Sosarme*, where his libretto borrows a text from a source with which he is known to have been acquainted; he is more likely than the poet to have suggested this. Eisenschmidt was the first to point out that additional or substituted arias inserted in the London librettos, especially those by Haym, conform to a definite pattern. The majority of them have a powerful emotional content, giving direct expression to grief, longing, remorse or some other passion. They often replace decorative or neutral pieces, vague generalisations, far-fetched similes, and mythological metaphors — the space-fillers that formed the staple fare of pasticcios. By the same token, they offer enlarged opportunities for characterisation. Since an instant response to concrete rather than abstract imagery is one of the most striking features of Handel's style at all periods, and in view of his profound interest in all the workings of human nature, there is a strong probability that these new texts were included at his instigation. Sometimes the autographs confirm this. The

most famous and one of the most dramatically potent arias in *Rodelinda*, 'Dove sei?', occurs neither in the source libretto nor in Handel's first draft; he inserted it during one of his revisions, and modified it more than once later. It is impossible to believe that, had it been present in Haym's original text, Handel would have left it out, or that Haym would have supplied it unasked. The autographs tell us a great deal about Handel's struggles with his librettos; {...} The most remarkable instance is afforded by *Tamerlano*: after composing the entire opera to one libretto, Handel incorporated large sections of another on the same subject only weeks or even days before the performance, and continued to make major alterations up to the last moment.[110]

Rolli may have displayed a resistance to Handel's alterations, as he was a follower of Zeno's reforms promoting the reduction of arias and the inclusion of more recitatives. Texts by the Arcadian librettists such as Zeno and Metastasio were not sources of inspiration for Handel, and when he eventually set their librettos, they were dramatically altered. From the listing of productions in Appendix Two, operas where the earlier sources may be traced and were based on those of Zeno number approximately seven. Rolli adapted more Zeno texts than Haym; Rolli adapted four Zeno texts, while Haym adapted three. Handel set only one Zeno text compiled by Rolli, and one from Haym. Handel also set the only Metastasio text for the Royal Academy in collaboration with Haym. Therefore, Handel composed music for only three out of the eight texts originally written by these two Arcadian masters, and two of these texts were adapted by Haym. Strikingly, the Zeno and the Metastasio texts Handel set by Haym are either pasticcios, or were adaptations of earlier music; Handel probably approached Haym

---

[110] Ibid. pp. 17–18.

concerning the adaptation of these texts due to Haym's co-operative nature.

This "mutilation" of the Arcadians' masterpieces was a particular issue with Rolli's clique. We may trace this conflict in the listing of Appendix Two as many of the Arcadian-member texts were allocated to composers who were Arcadian sympathisers. Bononcini set more librettos with Rolli in contrast to the limited number he set for Haym: six Rolli-librettos in contrast to Haym's two librettos. In addition, two of the librettos complied by Rolli for Bononcini are based on originals by Zeno; Rolli adapted only one Zeno text for Handel. Perhaps the most intriguing information concerns Bononcini who dedicated the libretto of *Farnace* (1723) to the Earl of Peterborough, and may have organised the text.[111] Traditionally, composers did not dedicate a libretto, however, Handel included a dedication with *Radamisto*[112] during the early days of the Academy, and it would appear that Bononcini was imitating Handel's actions. In addition, we may observe an important incident that adversely affected the Italians — Haym replaced Rolli as Italian Secretary of the Royal Academy for the last six seasons.[113] Bononcini wrote his dedication during Haym's second year as Secretary; perhaps this

---

[111] Deutsch, p. 155.

[112] Ibid. p. 103.

[113] Taylor, *Italian Operagoing*, p. 114. See also the article by Lowell Lindgren, 'The Accomplishments of the Learned and Ingenious Nicola Francesco Haym (1678-1729)' in *Studi Musicali*, Anno XVI – No. 2 (Firenze: 1987): pp. 304–305 concerning Haym's appointment. Lindgren surmises that Rolli may have been dismissed due to his indignation on account of the suppression of Catholics initiated by Robert Walpole in spring of 1721. Walpole had instigated various anti-papist and anti-Jacobite campaigns, thus Roman Catholics in general were demoted or deprived of certain liberties. In 1722–1723, Rolli and Bononcini were offered a reduced salary because of these events; Rolli could have refused to accept such treatment and may have been released from his position as Italian Secretary to the Academy as a result.

action reveals Bononcini's protest to this situation.

The fact that the musician / composer Handel and Haym were united as a "Dynamic Duo", and obviously obtaining control over the literary aspect of opera production, may have proved intolerable to Rolli and his Italian cohorts. It was insufferable that Haym, who was not considered "a man of letters" by them,[114] was co-operating with Handel and apparently was submissive to his text alterations and close involvement. Could this have disturbed the process of the "Arcadian plan"? The idea that the English accepted these deviations from the Italian tradition was beyond endurance. This refers to the issue of English assimilation where less importance was placed on having "authentic" productions perfect to the last detail. Haym's succession after Rolli is evidence of this as Taylor points out Haym was ideally suited to the office of Secretary according to English expectations:

> As in the first two decades, {i.e. of the 1700s,} the Secretary of the Academy was a professional who combined literary and musical with managerial responsibilities. He adapted Italian librettos by adjusting the balance of recitative and aria from the originals to suit the resident performers and English taste. {...} There are exceptions, but it was generally in the name of the Secretary, not the composer, that the libretto was dedicated to a patron (or patrons as applicable.) Production and management rather than poetic responsibilities probably occupied the bulk of the Secretary's time. It was his responsibility, in cooperation with the music director, to ascertain that the work materialized onstage. {...}
> He {Haym} had an ability "to accommodate everyone's wishes, prepare the accommodation for the

---

[114] Dorris, Italian Circle, p. 82.

printer, then serve as the stage director."* Rolli, by contrast, seems to have been a rather resentful character who entertained loftier literary and social ambitions than his circumstances and perhaps his talent allowed.[115]

We discover through contemporaneous documents that the Italians who comprised the "Inner core" of the circle were displeased with the procedures by which Italian opera was produced in England. Lindgren quotes Rolli's complaints concerning this situation, stating that:

> In 1724, he expressed his displeasure with those Academicians {i.e., the Royal Academy Academicians}, whose "lack of caring and economy solely on the intellectual part of the operas" had resulted in their employment of "Idiots and bad craftsmen, {who} are inexhaustible sources of Nonsense."[116]

Two of Riva's surviving letters to the Arcadian Muratori also state disappointment with the policies conducted in England:

Hanover, 7th September 1725.

> The operas performed in England, fine though they are as regards the music and the voices, are so

---

* Taylor's footnote: "From Lowell Lindgren, 'The Accomplishments of Nicola Francesco Haym,' p. 308 and *passim*."

[115] Taylor, *Italian Operagoing*, pp. 113–114.

[116] Rolli's remarks are printed in *Gli amanti interni; commedia inglese del cavaliere Riccardo Steele*, trans. and ed. Paolo Rolli (London: 1724), pp. 163–164, in 'The Accomplishments of Nicola Francesco Haym,' p. 306. The translation is my own; "non curanza ed economia sulla sole parte intellettuale delle Opere" — "Idioti e Guastamestieri, inesauste fonti di Nonsenso."

much hackwork as regards the verses. Our friend Rolli, who was commissioned to compose them when the Royal Academy was first formed, wrote really good operas, but having become embroiled with the Directors, the latter took into their service one Haym, a Roman and a violoncellist, who is a complete idiot as far as Letters are concerned. Boldly passing from the orchestra to the heights of Parnassus, he has, for the last three years, been adapting — or rather making worse — the old librettos which are already bad enough in their original form. The *Capellmeisters*, who compose the operas, make use of these, with the exception of our compatriot Bononcino, who has sent for his [librettos] from Rome, they are being composed by certain pupils of Gravina. If your friend wishes to send some, he must know that in England they want few recitatives, but thirty arias and one duet at least, distributed over the three acts. The subject-matter must be straightforward, tender, heroic, Roman, Greek, or even Persian, and never Gothic or Longobard. {...} From this, your friend will be able to obtain an idea of the sort of operas which can serve in England.[117]

Kensington, 2nd October 1726.

All my readiness to obey you in the matter of the Opera, which you say will be sent to me by post will be in vain, because the composers of Music have already chosen the librettos for the coming season and are already at work on them. It will also be difficult to have it accepted for the first year after, because the Academy

---

[117] Deutsch, pp. 185–186.

have their own poet, {i.e. Haym,} and operas that come from Italy cannot be of service in this theatre. It is necessary to revise or rather deform them in order to render them acceptable. Few verses of recitative and many arias is what they want over here, and that is the reason why it has never been possible to perform some of Signor Apostolo's* best operas [librettos] and why Metastasio's two finest operas, that is to say his *Dido* and *Siroe*, have met the same fate. Besides, there are more poets here than are required; in addition to the Academy's poet, there is Rolli, and one Brillanti from Pistoia, who manages very well. All the others remain idle, so that for your friend to make the journey here, would be both expensive and useless. That is what I am able to tell you, Sir, on this matter.[118]

Riva laments that several Arcadian masterpieces met their demise at the Academy as they were edited beyond recognition compliments of Haym's intervention. Intriguingly, Bononcini no longer trusted the Academy to supply "appropriate" librettos and preferred to commission the pupils of the Arcadian Gravina in Italy, thereby securing authentic Arcadian products rather than resort to librettos "malformed" by English expectations. In fact, one of Rolli's most interesting remarks regarding his own works, that his librettos were "dramatic skeletons," may refer to the curtailment of recitative expected by the English.[119]

Apparently, the Arcadians were completely abhorred by this "deplorable" situation. All aspects of the Royal Academy were operating in opposition to their ideals; Handel, a composer, was more important than the poets, librettos were "deformed," and the

---

* I.e. Zeno's librettos.

[118] Deutsch, p. 197.

[119] Dorris, *Italian Circle*, p. 167. (Reference to a primary source not mentioned by Dorris.)

English were quite content. Furthermore, the issue pertaining to the setting of librettos was just a singular aspect of these disagreements.

Handel, in his consideration of scenic display and drama, composed his music in such a manner that it assisted the portrayal of action; this may have been an extremely sensitive point with the Arcadian Italians. There is evidence to support the theory he allowed the music to encroach upon the literary aspect of the drama, which would have provoked a reaction from the Italians. Handel agreed and proceeded to comply with the English demand for less recitatives and an increased number of arias; he allowed the music to serve as the dramatic conduit. He used his music to assume part of the dramatic function of the recitatives, and was equally inventive with his arias as he was inspired by emotional situations and excelled in this area — the *da capo* aria was Handel's playground. Hypothetically, Arcadian Italians would have opposed Handel's musical contributions to the drama. Dean offers several examples concerning Handel's techniques.

Handel often melded recitative with his arias; he would juxtapose these two elements without a cadence, or he would incorporate recitative within the aria structure.[120] Dean mentions we may observe these techniques within *Giulio Cesare*. With the aria "Dall' ondoso periglio," the accompanied recitative returns in the middle of the aria, and through thematic reference, the design is bound together.[121] In some cases, another character interrupts the second part of a *da capo* by introducing recitative, e.g, when Caesar utters an exclamation at the beauty of Cleopatra's "V'adoro pupille."[122] [See Example 1.]

---

[120] Dean, *Opera Seria*. p. 169.
[121] Ibid.
[122] Ibid.

Example I

"V'adoro" from *Giulio Cesare*
A Section, Bars 1–7.

B Section, Bars 40–47. Followed by Cesar's recitative.

(B Section; Bars 40–47)

(Cesar's interrupting recitative).

Dean observes that Handel may have been ahead of his contemporaries with regard to his practise of "dissolving" the recitative-aria alternation pattern. A significant number of his operas contain scenes where this pattern is disrupted and the music continues for several movements. Dean states, "His care for dramatic values led him to modify the formal scheme to express not only states of mind but character in action, and here most of all the stiffness of the convention enabled him to bring off all manner of surprises. This begins very early in his career."[123] This manipulation of recitative, the main conduit for dramatic action, would assuredly have been a contentious issue with the Arcadians.

Continuing with Handel's development of the *da capo* aria, Dean mentioned:

> The more closely we examine the da capo aria with Handel, the more flexible and less stereotyped it appears. Take for example, the opening ritornello. More often than not this prefigures the first phrase or melody sung by the voice. But the voice may treat it differently or introduce something new, which can be contrasted or combined with the ritornello. In arias expressing emotional conflict the ritornello may present ideas of dissimilar or seemingly incompatible type, sometimes with a change of tempo or rhythm, and the voice may develop one, both or neither of them. {…}
>
> There is no knowing in advance at what stage, if ever, the voice will take up any of the ideas of the ritornello, which may of course be suited only to instrumental treatment. Handel's delight and ours, consists in a perpetual teasing and baffling of the expectation of the ear. One simple but unfailing effective stroke is to make the voice overlap the ritornello by entering, perhaps with a sustained note, before the completion of its cadence. [124]

---

[123] Ibid. p.171.
[124] Ibid. pp.157–158.

{For example — Asteria's aria at the end of Act II in *Tamerlano*, see Example 2.}

Example 2

Asteria's aria "Se potessi un di placare" from *Tamerlano*.

Bars 1–28.

Dean also notes that Handel in certain instances omitted or postponed the ritornello:

> If the aria represents an immediate reaction to a

question or a threat, it may interrupt the recitative cadence. Instead of waiting for the orchestra the voice enters at once, to suggest urgency or indignation. The ritornello may follow when the singer pauses for breath, or it may be withheld until the da capo, when it will alter the balance of the aria. A suppressed ritornello can convey gentler emotions. {...}"[125]

Dean also brings to our attention Handel's use of tonality that appears inconsequential on paper, but is aurally surprising. Dean offers the aria "Non disperi peregrino" at the end of Act II of *Lotario* as one example, "Handel moves from the tonic, E flat, into the dominant, but in such a devious manner, with feints into F minor and G minor, that he creates a sense of bold harmonic adventure, intensified later by a glimpse of E flat minor at the end of the first part."[126] In other arias, Handel employed modulations that involved major and minor thirds, as Dean observes with Radamisto's aria "Ferite, uccidite", " ... the ritornello sideslips from A major into C major, changing the key signature for fifteen bars."[127] Of notable interest, Dean states these modulations involving thirds are characteristic of the early Romantic period, adding that when "Handel uses them, unprepared, to make a dramatic point, they have a powerful emotional impact that inevitably strikes us as romantic." [128] In addition, Dean describes Handel's orchestration:

{...} The orchestra is never a mere background or cradle for the voice — it supplies the atmosphere in which the music breaths and draws its lifeblood. Three characteristics of Handel's practise may be singled out;

---

[125] Ibid.
[126] Ibid. pp. 164–165.
[127] Ibid.
[128] Ibid.

the wide scope, both in instrument choice and in their various blends and permutations; the intimate relationship with the dramatic context; and the feeling for the timbre and texture, based on the instinctive understanding of the instruments and an infallible ear. {...} Taken as a whole, Handel's scoring is richer than that of his opera seria contemporaries (the charge of noisiness is proof of this) and may to some extent reflect the lasting influence of the Hamburg school, especially Keiser, who was fond of picturesque accompaniments. {...} In opera and oratorio alike Handel did employ a wide range of instrumental color, even for an age when the orchestra was not standardized and obsolescent instruments like the theorbo and viola da gamba persisted alongside new inventions like the clarinet.[129]

Handel incorporated stage and curtain effects in conjunction with the music. Dean notes this area requires further study, but there are various indications in the music that may relate to scenery and stage directions.[130] In some instances, Handel composed specifically for the scene changes, for example the instrumental music in Act I of *Radamisto* was intended to accompany action, i.e. the attack upon the city, and was not intended to be heard as an interlude.[131] We may also observe Act I of *Alessandro* is similar, as the sinfonia of scene one continues into scene two and accompanies the action where Alexander's soldiers arrive with a battering ram to destroy the city walls. For other scenes that did not feature "linking music", tonality was used to indicate the change of scenery.[132] Handel also experimented with the practise of raising and lowering

---

[129] Ibid. p. 185–186.
[130] Ibid. p. 123.
[131] Ibid. p. 128.
[132] Ibid.

the stage curtain. According to Baroque *opera seria* convention, the lowering of the curtain did not take place between the acts as they performed the scene changes in full view of the audience to incite wonder. However, Handel experimented with the raising of the curtain at unexpected moments; for instance, he tricked the audience with several of his French overtures by allowing the last movement of the overture to overlap or "act" as the first scene indicating that the curtain must have been raised earlier.[133] Dean also theorises that Handel specifically composed the two or three measures following the final *coro* to accommodate the lowering of the curtain while the singers took their bows.[134]

In additon, Handel eliminated a variety of conventions in a number of his operas, such as the "exit" convention where the singer leaves the stage after performing their aria. According to Dean, several contemporary librettists such as Metastasio preferred to commence a scene with recitative while others, especially those influenced by Venetian traditions, introduced a scene with a full aria. Handel avoided these concepts when possible and commenced an act with an arioso or a sinfonia thereby allowing additional scope for structural possibilities. Dean states, "With an arioso, the 'exit' convention was not required and like a sinfonia it could be used to build up a climax later in the scene."[135]

It is possible that Handel's practises created enmity or a significant degree of friction with the Arcadians considering how they regarded music and scenography within *opera seria* as the least important components. In addition, Handel's insistence for control with the production of his operas also influenced traditions surrounding the status of the principle singers, and this would prove intolerable to the Italians.

We have already noted Handel's rigid approach with Senesino — this attitude also extended to other singers as he

---

[133] Ibid. pp.123–124, 130.
[134] Ibid. p.125.
[135] Ibid. p. 42.

endeavoured to maintain control over the various proceedings. Handel upheld his personal convictions concerning characterisation, and when composing an opera he infrequently allowed interaction from the singers, which was anti-Arcadian; for instance, he rarely permitted a principal singer to incorporate arias from their repertory, thereby dismissing an accepted custom, and seldom allowed them to influence any of his decisions concerning the arias. An example of his unyielding nature is displayed with the amusing anecdote describing the incident when Handel threatened to throw the singer Cuzzoni out of the window upon her refusal to sing "Falsa imagine" in *Ottone* (1723).[136]

Handel created specific character roles according to the skills of the various singers,[137] and this may explain his controlling attitude and his involvement with the libretto revisions. Larue maintains that Handel observed no particular character style with Durastanti or Senesino according to the roles he assigned to them,[138] while with others such as Cuzzoni, Handel noticed her skill in portraying a particular style of character. Handel set a number of Cuzzoni's characters as pathetic-heroines, reflecting her ability for musical expression of pathos;[139] in fact, this may explain the major disagreement concerning the choice of arias for her in *Ottone*.[140] Larue presents evidence that *Ottone* was originally intended for

---

[136] See Mainwaring, f. on p. 110.

[137] See C. Stephen Larue's book *Handel and his Singers; The Creation of the Royal Academy Operas, 1720–1728*, (Oxford: Clarendon Press, 1995) concerning the association of singers with certain character roles.

[138] Ibid. pp. 83–84, 107, 115. This may explain why Handel possibily suggested Durastanti for the Academy — she was capable of filling several character roles and thereby would allow him more freedom with the setting of opera librettos.

[139] Ibid. p. 138.

[140] The first performance of *Ottone* was on January 12th, 1723. Deutsch, p. 147.

Durastanti, and not Cuzzoni.[141] Cuzzoni may have objected to performing arias for her debut in London initially intended for another prima donna, and apparently construed this presentation of "second-hand" material as an insult. However, Larue quotes Burney who observed that the very arias Handel would not change made Cuzzoni renowned for her style as a pathetic heroine:

> The Slow air, *Falsa imagine,* the first which
> Cuzzoni sung in this country, fixed her reputation as an
> expressive and pathetic singer; as *Affanni del pensier* did
> Handel's, as a composer of such songs. (Burney).[142]

If this famous "window" anecdote is indeed true, Handel possibly objected to Cuzzoni's refusal perhaps to avoid unnecessary revision time, or, he recognised her musical capabilities and deduced changing the opera was not particularly necessary. As mentioned previously, librettos portraying emotional possibilities inspired Handel, and therefore he may have considered Cuzzoni quite suitable, or better qualified, for the role he had intended for Durastanti. Mainwaring observed that throwing someone out of a window was a contemporary method of execution in several parts of Germany — perchance Handel viewed Cuzzoni's refusal as a crime against his artistic creativity and therefore deserving of capital punishment.

Obviously, Handel defended his right as composer to remain involved with the creative process of his work, such as the development of the emotional aspects of the characters within his music, and was defiant with those who questioned his authority; this is evident in two letters written by Anastasia Robinson. She believed she was not equal to the role Handel had composed for her in *Ottone*; in fact, she was petrified to approach him upon this

---

[141]   See Larue, *Handel and his Singers,* pp. 98–102.

[142]   Charles Burney, *A General History of Music* (London: 1776–89):
p. 722, in Larue, *Handel and hs Singers,* p. 101.

subject and wrote to Riva enquiring if he would act as her emissary. These two surviving letters are a fascinating exposé of Handel's customary lack of diplomacy towards the singers:

Now I want your advice for my self, you have hear'd my new Part, and the more I look at it, the more I find it impossible for me to sing it; I dare not ask Mr. Hendell to change the Songs for fear he should suspect (as he is very likely) every other reason but the true one. Do you believe if I was to wait on Lady Darlington to beg her to use that power over him (which to be sure she must have,) to get it done, that she would give her self that trouble, would she have so much compassion on a distressed Damsell that they are endeavouring to make an abbomminable Scold of (in spite of her Virtuous inclinations to the contrary) as to hinder the wrong they would do her; you might be my friend and represent, tho the greatest part of my Life has shew'd me to be a Patient Grisell by Nature, how then can I ever pretend to act the Termagant. But to speak seriously I desire you tell me whether it would be wrong to beg my Lady Darlington to do me this very great favour, and you think should do it, for Sr your obliged humble Servant

Anastasia Robinson

Sr

Not knowing how to ask you to give your self the trouble of coming here, and the necessity obliging me to beg a favour of you, I must do it by writing. I am very sensible the Musick of my Part is extremely fine, but am as sure the Caracter causes it to be of that kind, which no way suits my Capacity: those Songs that

90

require fury and passion to express them, can never be performed by me according to the intention of the Composer, and consequently must loose their Beauty. Nature designed me a peaceable Creature, and it is as true as strange, that I am a Woman and can-not Scold. My request is, that if it be possible (as it sure is) the words of my Second Song Pensa spietata Madre should be changed, and instead of reviling Gismonda with her cruelty, to keep on the thought of the Recitative and perswade her to beg her Sons life of Ottone. I have read the Drama and tho I do not pretend to be a judge, yet I fancy doing this would not be an impropriety, but even supposing it one, of two evills it is best to chuse the least; in this manner you might do me the greatest favour imaginable, because a Short Melancholly Song would be proper. I have some dificultys allso in the last I Sing, but for fear that by asking too much I might be refus'd all, I dare not mention them. And now I beg of you to believe no other motive induces me to give you this trouble, but the fear I have that it would be impossible for me to perform my Part tollerably. By your granting what I so exstreamly desire, I shall have a double satisfaction, being gratify'd in what I insist on, and the pleasure of knowing you to be a real Friend to she who is Sr your obliged humble servant

Anastasia Robinson[143]

Interestingly, Robinson concluded if she requested him to alter her role, Handel would become suspicious; obviously, he was mistrustful of the singers' demands. Moreover, she mentions her

---

[143] From Edition der Hallischen Händel-Ausgabe, *Händel-Handbuch*, iv. Dokument zu Leben und Schaffen (Kassel: Bärenreiter, 1985), pp. 112–113, in Larue, *Handel and his Singers*, pp. 125–126.

anxiety to perform her part *"according to the intention of the Composer."*[144]   Handel's interest in creating character parts with emotional integration with his music apparently had been noticed by one singer, and may have been observed by other performers; this certainly displays an important change in the status of the composer's role.   This also clarifies Handel's "hard-fisted" attitude towards the singers; if they could insert their *aria di baule* into an opera or disagree with the music he was composing for them, the overall intention he had wished to portray through their characters might be undone.   Additionally, this would require extra time to reset the texts if he condescended to their requests.   In lieu of diplomatically wasting time with explanations, it was expedient for him to display his autocratic nature and play the heavy disciplinarian, further antagonising the Arcadian Italians.   Mainwaring asserts that Handel's insistence on controlling the singers, particularly Senesino, created the most critical predicament the Academy would endure:

> SENESINO, who, from his first appearance, had taken deep root, and had long been growing in the affections of those, whose right to dominion the most civilized nations have ever acknowledged, began to feel his strength and importance.   He felt them so much, that what he had hitherto regarded as legal government, now appeared to him in the light of downright tyranny. HANDEL, perceiving that he was grown less tractable and obsequious, resolved to subdue these Italian humours, not by lenitives, but by sharp corrosives.   To *manage* him he disdained; to controul him with a high-hand, he in vain attempted.   The one was perfectly refractory; the other was equally outrageous.   In short, matters had proceeded so far, that there was no

---

[144]   Handel must have been sympathetic to Robinson's plea, for according to Larue, Handel considered her suggestions.   See Larue, *Handel and his Singers*, pp. 129–130.

accommodation.[145]

Handel was self-promoting his position of authority within the Academy by asserting control of the singers, who according to traditional conventions could exert more influence concerning the production of opera, and this may explain why Senesino refused to "submit" as Mainwaring relates. It was unfortunate that Handel and Senesino did not reach a compromise, for their feud had devastating consequences during the "Second" Academy.

We have observed that several problems continued to haunt the duration of the Royal Academy. Handel was protective of his position as the Academy's composer, including various aspects of his work that clashed with the Italians' Arcadian aesthetics. Handel was involved with the text setting and preferred to work with Haym, considered by the other Italians as a mediocre librettist. Handel also incorporated the drama of the operas into his music thus illustrating his co-operation with English expectations regarding opera production. Finally, he displayed a tyrannical attitude with regard to the singers traditionally considered more important than the composer. A managerial collapse was inevitable, and the feud pertaining to the singers would prove to be the breaking point, as we shall discover.

The Closure of the Royal Academy

Mainwaring marks the troubles between the rival prima donnas Cuzzoni and Faustina Bordoni[146] as the deciding factor in the final closure of the Royal Academy:

FAUSTINA and CUZZONI, as if seized with

---

[145] Mainwaring, pp. 107–108.
[146] Faustina Bordoni had arrived in 1726.

the contagion of discord, started questions of superiority, and urged their respective claims to it with eagerness and acrimony, which occasioned a total disunion betwixt them.

And thus the Academy, after it had continued in the most flourishing state for upwards of nine years, was at once dissolved.[147]

However, how could a dispute between two singers cause such a collapse? This incident alone is inconclusive. If we combine this event with the other factions that were corroding the Academy internally, this incident may have been the proverbial last straw.

Notwithstanding the rivalry involving the composers from the time of *Muzio Scevola*, it appears the directors were continually in dissension. Surviving evidence dating from earlier years also demonstrates the persistent competition between the dissenters and their supporters:

Monsieur de Fabrice to Count Flemming
(Translated)

London, January 15th, 1722–23.

{...} Over and above that, there exist two factions, the one supporting Hendell, the other Bononcini, the one for Cenesino and the other for Cossuna. They are as much at loggerheads as the Whigs and Tories, and even on occasion sow dissension among the directors.[148]

The next example of internal discordance occurs with the

---

147 Mainwaring, p. 109.
148 Deutsch, pp. 147–148.

rehearsal of Ariosti's *Vespasiano*, indicating that these problems may be related to the differences in artistic tastes and expectations. Could the Italians and their clique have been involved in the following disputes?

From Mist's "Weekly Journal", 18th January 1724

> We hear there have been strange Comotions in the State of Musick in the Opera-House in the Hay-Market, and that a civil Broil arose among the Subscribers at the Practise of the new Opera of *Vespasian*, which turn'd all the Harmony into Discord; and that if these Dissentions do not cease, it is thought *Opera* Stock will fall.[149]

Next, we have a peculiar letter describing a performance of Handel's *Giulio Cesare*:

John Byrom to His Wife Elizabeth, 3rd March 1724

> I was engaged to dine at Mrs. de Vlieger's on Saturday [29th February], whence they all went to the opera of Julius Caesar, and I for one. Mr. Leycester sat by me in the front row of the gallery, for we both were there to get good places betimes; it was the first entertainment of this nature that I ever saw, and I will hope be the last, for all the diversions of the town I least of all enter into this.[150]

This is a strange comment as this opera was one of Handel's most successful works during the Royal Academy. A letter written

---

[149]   Ibid. p. 157.
[150]   Ibid. p. 158.

by M. de Fabrice to Count Flemming describing a similar performance may clarify Byrom's disappointment:

London, March 10th, 1724.

... The opera is in full swing also, since Hendell's new one, called Jules César — in which Cenesino and Cozzuna shine beyond all criticism — has been put on. The house was just as full at the seventh performance as at the first. In addition to that the squabbles, between the Directors and the sides that everyone is taking between the singers and the composers, often provide the public with the most diverting scenes.[151]

Hence, we observe the use of the term "diverting scenes" to describe the uproars, making Byrom's letter understandable, e.g. "for all the diversions of the town," he does not wish to repeat this experience. It is interesting M. Fabrice mentions the directors first, proceeding with his account of the singers and composers, and finally the point that arguments had extended to the public domain. There is circumstantial evidence to suggest these "diversions" were due to the conflicts between Handel and the Italian group:

An Epistle to Mr. Handel,
Upon His Operas of Flavius and Julius Caesar

[7th March 1724]

{...} Some little *Rebels* to thy mighty Name,
Deny the Crown due justly to your Fame;
No Sons of *Phœbus*, but a purious Breed,

---

[151] Ibid. p. 160.

Who suck bad Air, and on thin Diet feed; {...}[152]

We sense that Rolli and his Italian sympathisers, the "Rebels" who were no "Sons of Phoebus," were involved with these problems. Later we observe John Byrom's well-known "Tweedle-dum" epigram appearing in May 1725 satirising the rivalries between Bononcini and Handel, which suggests the arguments between the supporters for the various composers had not diminished, originating with Handel's resistance to the Italians, and their disapproval of his production methods:

> Some say, compar'd to Bononcini,
> That Mynheer Handel's but a Ninny;
> Others aver, that he to Handel
> Is scarcely fit to hold a candle:
> Strange all this Difference should be
> 'Twixt Tweedle-dum and Tweedle-dee!

> John Byrom, *Epigram on the Feuds*
> *Between Handel and Bononcini*[153]

Finally, these problems climaxed after the arrival of Faustina in 1726, generating additional parties defending their favourite singers:

From the "British Journal", 10th June 1727

On Tuesday-night last [the 6th], a great Disturbance happened at the Opera, occasioned by the Partisans of the Two Celebrated Rival Ladies, Cuzzoni

---

[152] Ibid. p. 158–159.
[153] Deutsch, p. 180.

and Faustina. The contention at first was only carried on by Hissing on one Side, and Clapping on the other; but proceeded at length to Catcalls, and other Indecencies: And not withstanding the Princess Caroline was present, no Regards were of Force to restrain the Rudenesses of the Opponents.[154]

Unfortunately, this new disturbance also relates to the English issue of assimilation. The ambitious directors wished to assemble the best opera company possible, yet they remained oblivious to past experiences regarding the public's tendency to splinter into various supporting groups. The directors continued to mould an eclectic company:

From the "Flying Post", 4th February 1727.

The Directors of the Royal Academy of Musick have resolved, that after the Excellent Opera composed by Mr. Hendell, which is now performing; Signior Attilia shall compose one: And Signior Bononcini is to compose the next after that. Thus, as this Theatre can boast of the three best Voices in Europe, and the best Instruments; {…} this polite and Rich nation will by Collecting what is perfect out of various Countries, become the Place where all Travellers will stay to be diverted and instructed in this Science, as well as in others.[155]

Obviously, the directors did not consider the repercussion if a new singer arrived; this decision to hire Faustina created a catastrophic upheaval. During these latter years, we note additional

---

[154] Ibid. p. 210.
[155] Ibid. pp. 201–202.

lampooning and satires featuring the latest scandals of the Royal Academy flitting the papers of the day. A famous article, "The Contre Temps; or Rival Queens: a Small Farce," featured in the *Monthly Catalogue* of July 1727.[156] In this satire, Handel "animates" the infamous battle between the two "queens" Faustina and Cuzzoni with a kettledrum in front of "The Temple of Discord", an allegory of the Haymarket Theatre. (The two singers actually engaged in a physical battle onstage during a performance!) On a more serious note, many subscribers failed to answer the calls issued by the directors; apparently, the appeal and novelty for Italian opera eroded as a consequence of these disputes which exposed the enterprise to the cynics, rendering it vulnerable to additional criticism, particularly from the English genre supporters whose cause was subdued earlier before the Academy's foundation. With the production of the *Beggar's Opera* on January 29th, 1728,[*] Italian opera was slowly entering its sunset as noted by Mrs. Pendarves:

November 1727 and January 1728;

{...} I doubt operas will not survive longer than this winter, they are now at their last gasp; the subscription is expired and nobody will renew it. The directors are always squabbling, and they have so many divisions among themselves that I wonder they have not broke up before; Senesino goes away next winter, and I

---

[156] Ibid. p. 212.

[*] The Duchess of Queensbury supported this work by guaranteeing John Rich the expenses of its production. Dorris maintains that this was not an outward attack on Italian opera, as she was a firm supporter of Bononcini and the Italian group. In addition, there is no evidence that Gay was attempting to bankrupt Handel or that there had been a rift between them. Dorris also says; "The *Beggar's Opera* is comic, not vicious, the points well made, and the result good fun." See Dorris, *Italian Circle*, pp. 97–98.

believe Faustina, so you see harmony is almost out of fashion.[157]

Somerset House, 29th Jan. 1727–8.

Yesterday I was at the rehearsal of the new opera composed by Handel; I like it extremely, but the taste of the town is so depraved, that nothing will be approved of but the burlesque. The Beggars' Opera entirely triumphs over the Italian one.[158]

Hogwood points out that "The triumph of 'burlesque' was a result, rather than the cause of the Academy's collapse."[159] This observation is also applicable to the differences between Faustina and Cuzzoni; their public confrontation was the *result* of the previous escalating friction, and became the final step towards the company's dissolution. This unprofessional display was the ultimate example for those who perceived Italian opera as a frivolous, expensive, and perhaps outright laughable amusement. The public in general had grown weary of the unrelenting disputes and consequently this presented an opportunity for the development of an English genre to resurface. Although Italian opera would not fail until years later, production of this genre had re-entered a period of instability similar to that experienced in 1705–1719.

If Handel or the Italians had compromised, would the Academy have survived? Arguably, this would depend on the willingness of either faction to concede to English expectations. I hope it has been successfully established that the English preferred a more stylised and eclectic genre, and obviously Handel was

---

[157] Ibid. p. 218.
[158] Ibid. p. 220.
[159] Hogwood, *Handel*, p. 88.

considered the most qualified to accomplish this task; we may conclude the Academy would have survived if the Italians had been more tolerant and cooperative. However, they alternatively created a rift between their English patrons.

When we view the situation from this perspective, Handel's authoritarian approach with the production of opera at the Academy is completely comprehensible as it became vital to create a level of order and stability in that institution. The company's foundation apparently lacked foresight, and the directors and patrons were divided; how the Royal Academy continued to function with such internal turmoil defies our understanding. Perhaps Mainwaring's comment referred to earlier in Chapter One stating the Academy's demise was eminent from the beginning may hold more truth than previously realised. He suggests that Handel's:

> {...}perfect authority {...} or rather the total subjection in which he held them, was of more consequence than can be well imagined. It was the chief means of preserving that order and decorum, that union and tranquillity, which seldom are found to subsist for long continuance in musical Societies.[160]

However, it obviously would prove difficult for Handel to maintain a standard of stability indefinitely as the public had grown indifferent to the affairs of the Academy; despite the warnings issued concerning the threat of prosecution the supporters continually failed to answer the subscription calls, and attendance at the operas diminished. Finally, the Royal Academy folded on June 1st, 1728.

While the demand for Italian opera had not failed completely, the status that it once held was in decline and renewed interest in developing an English genre was resurfacing. The first important outlet available was through ballad opera ushered in by the *Beggar's*

---

[160] Mainwaring, pp. 106–107.

Opera. These two styles of opera would be vying for dominance; Italian opera production would be in competition with English genres yielding unusual results. In addition, many of the difficulties experienced within the Royal Academy would resume during the "Second" Academy under Handel and Heidegger's management. Next, we will explore this strained period concerning opera culture in London in an attempt to disclose the circumstances which led Handel to Covent Garden.

Chapter 3

The "Second" Academy:
Handel's Opportunity for Control

In 1728, plans to salvage the opera company were in the formative stages. Ironically, the directors continued to assemble as the "Academy" despite the fact the venture was dormant at that point; perhaps this is an indication of the state of confusion that existed and displays the aftermath of "The Artistic Wars" of the Royal Academy.

Documents suggest the former directors were finding it difficult to pick up the pieces and could not find a solution to the previous rancour. Therefore, they initially proceeded to reorganize using a similar administrative formula that they had previously used to establish the Royal Academy. On December 8th, 1728, a notice was published in the *London Gazette* announcing the time had come, as stipulated in the Charter of the Royal Academy, to elect the new Deputy Governor and directors.[161] Rolli wrote a letter describing the plans to re-establish the company to Senesino who was currently in Venice; apparently, Handel once again received the commission to engage new singers as Rolli reported Handel spoke well of Farinelli, (Carlo Broschi). Rolli's letter also illustrates the public continued to support the previous singers and disputed their merits despite the fact these performers had departed England when the company collapsed:

---

[161] Deutsch, p. 229.

L. [London], 21st December [1728?]

{...} The Man [Handel] returned from his travels very full of Farinello and extremely loud in his praises. The parties of the two prima donas here are still green-eyed and watchful (*in viridi observantia*); and each side wants to have its way, so much so that to put the Opera again on its feet, they have finally decided to have both ladies back. The Man, my good friend, did not want this, but as the ladies have two parties and my friend Senesino has only one, so on that matter there was no other answer but that Senesino must be the first singer. Cuzzona is in his favour, Faustina is for herself and for him besides, Senesino is for everybody. They were wondering about the Impresario but it appears that the Man refuses to undertake the task and I am of the opinion that the Academy will, because that body is not yet dissolved. {...}[162]

This excerpt certainly brings to our attention a familiar situation reminiscent of the previous dissensions. In an effort to eliminate one obvious problem, the directors offered the position of impresario to Handel for this new venture. Strikingly, he rejected their offer; we know he would assume the position later with Heidegger, the manager of the Haymarket Theatre, so this raises the question of why he would initially refuse this opportunity. Judging from Rolli's letter, Handel was very apprehensive with the proposal to re-engage the prima donnas Cuzzoni and Faustina for the new company, concerned that unfortunate experiences from the past would have an opportunity to reoccur. Perhaps Handel decided not

---

[162] Ibid. pp. 229–230.

to assume the responsibility for this uncomfortable situation.

Resulting from Handel's objection, the directors had to reconsider and formulate alternative plans for their opera productions, and were open to new proposals for the venture. In a notice printed in the *London Gazette* on the 14th January 1729, the directors had called a general meeting:

> {…} in order to consider some Proposals that will then be offered for carrying on Operas; as also for disposing of the Effects belonging to the said Academy. [163]

Handel agreed with these new arrangements; according to Viscount Percival, Handel and Heidegger were "permitted" to carry on the operas "without disturbance for five years" with free use of all the Academy equipment. [164] The word "permitted" suggests that Handel and Heidegger did indeed arrange their own business agreements as Mainwaring states:

> The agreement was for the short term of three years, and so settled as to subsist only from year to year. [165]

Handel and Heidegger had provisionally agreed to attempt a joint venture, possibly for three years, which they apparently extended to five years when the directors had granted them exclusive use of the theatre stock. The nature of Heidegger and Handel's contract will be examined in more detail later as this had an important bearing on Handel's future relocation.

Noticeably, the aristocrats were not prepared to assume an active role in the company, (for the present); perhaps they had

---

[163] Ibid. p. 234.

[164] Ibid.

[165] Mainwaring, pp. 112–113.

exhausted themselves with their disputes, or simply the novelty of managing an opera company had worn thin. An intriguing observation, Handel and Heidegger, upon the acceptance of their proposal, were permitted to act as the managers while the nobility removed themselves from the day-to-day administrative duties of the re-established company. It seems they had recognised the stalemate concerning the previous management of the Royal Academy; by allowing Handel and Heidegger to act as managers suggests a reassessment of company policy, or maybe the directors decided to compromise in an effort to keep the venture afloat.

However, the various parties on behalf of the singers and composers continued to support their particular agendas, and consequently Heidegger decided to acquire a lucrative subscription by complying with their demands to re-engage Cuzzoni, Faustina, and Senesino. Handel was displeased with Heidegger's capitulation; this becomes apparent through Rolli's letter to Senesino on the 25th of January 1729:

> Heydeger returned and said that he had not found any singers in Italy; he protested that he did not wish to undertake anything without the two ladies; he spoke only of them and of Farinello. In the end, hearing that your friends desired you back, he gave way, and you are once more on good terms with him. He was thinking of a lucrative subscription than anything else and he was calculating well, for in this way the two parties and your friends in each would be helping to fill up the annual subscription with 20 pounds per head. This was the same, on the basis of which, already known to you, I wrote you the first letter. But Handel was not to be duped by such a paltry stratagem. He revealed his rival's rascally deceit: the only aim of his useless and ridiculous voyage was to profit himself alone. So he [Handel] declared that there was a need for change and has renewed the old system of changing

the singers in order to have the opportunity of composing new works for new performers. His new plans find favour at Court and he is satisfied. They want Farinello and Cuzzona, if she does not remain in Vienna, and the promoters are such as can pay. Mylord Bingley is at the head of the project, but the theatre has still to be found. So they called Heydeger and they granted him 2200 pounds with which to provide the theatre, the scenery and the costumes. {...}

That is the new system. Riva is already suffering from it, for you can well see what a very ill wind is blowing for Bononcino. {...}[166]

Handel would not accept Heidegger's scheme, and he re-established the "old system" of changing singers with the pretext it would afford him the opportunity to compose fresh material. Consequently, he presented his case before the Court to assure Royal support with his particular programme. Handel apparently had an ulterior motive for reinstating this system; obviously, he was reluctant to work with the same singers as they had proved to be too troublesome in the past. This also supports the previous observation that Handel initially refused to become the impresario as the dissentient Academy singers were being reconsidered for this new company.

This resulted in Handel obtaining additional control concerning the musical aspect of the Second Academy; he now had the authority to hire singers and other composers who met with his approval. Accordingly, the Arcadian Italians were already grumbling with this current state of affairs and were concerned for their beloved Bononcini, whom they feared would be excluded from this new venture:

---

[166] Deutsch, p. 235.

L. [London], 4th February 1729.

{…}The new Handeleidegriano [Handel-Heidegger] system is gaining ground. A general meeting was held and it was discussed. {…}

Riva is furious, because he sees Bononcino excluded by his own pride and by that of the Chief Composer {Handel}, on whom everything else will have to depend.[167]

Finally, Handel had obtained control, and this is evident from the new productions offered during the period of the Second Academy. (See Appendix Three.) Seven of the new operas were pasticcios if we include the last year Handel remained at the Haymarket; obviously, this is quite a substantial number of pasticcios for that short length of time when compared with the number he wrote for the Royal Academy. (See Appendix Four.) Handel may have been restricted regarding pasticcio compilations within the Royal Academy when Senesino refused Handel's suggestion that Polani compile the pasticcio based upon *Amore e Maestà*. In addition, Haym had died in 1729, and Handel's known librettist during this period, Samuel Humphreys, may not have been associated with the Italian circle and this probably facilitated Handel's pasticcio productions of the Arcadian masters Zeno and Metastasio. If Rossi was Handel's librettist for certain works as previously suspected,[168] he too was not a member of the "Inner" Italian circle,[169] and his co-operation with Handel may have supplied

---

[167]   Ibid. pp. 236–237.

[168]   See Rolli's letter to Riva, September 3rd, 1729 in Deutsch, p. 245.

[169]   Dorris states that Rolli may have disliked Haym because he was involved with the English attempts at producing a national opera style with Steele in opposition to the fledgling Italian circle. See Dorris, *Italian*

the Italians with an additional excuse to criticize his management.

However, Handel was not completely at liberty in certain areas despite the unparalleled control he had been granted concerning the musical proceedings. He was obliged to consider the preferences of his subscribers as they paid the expenses. Hence, we observe the librettos of Zeno and Metastasio were not abandoned entirely at this point; the English desire to assimilate the best in Italian culture apparently had to be recognised. In addition, Handel was eventually forced to capitulate to the demand for Senesino's return[170] as the public became dissatisfied with his choice of the castrato Bernacchi as we observe from Mrs. Pendarves and Rolli's letters:

Mrs. Pendarves to Her Sister, Ann Granville

Saturday Morning, 6 Dec. 1729.

{...} Bernacchi, the most famous of the men, is not approved of; he is certainly a good singer, but does not suit the English ears. {...}[171]

Rolli to Riva in Vienna (Translated)

London, 20th, [or rather, 11th?]

December 1729.

Nine days ago the opera *Lotario* was produced.

Circle, p. 143. It is possible Rolli also disapproved of Rossi, as he worked with Handel and Hill with the anglicization process of *Rinaldo*.

[170] Senesino returned in October 1730. See Deutsch, p. 260.

[171] Deutsch, p. 249.

I went only last Tuesday [the 9th], that is to the third performance. Everyone considers it a very bad opera. Bernacchi failed to please on the first night, but at the second performance he changed his method and scored a success. In person and voice he does not please as much as Senesino, but his great reputation as an artist silences those who cannot find it in them to applaud him. The truth is that he has only one aria in which he can shine, because ... he has blundered in the opera as a whole. {...}[172]

However, the opera itself was not a failure notwithstanding Rolli and his associates' opinions. Bernacchi seemingly "failed to please" the English. Eventually, the public's attention was diverted to other genres as Mrs. Pendarves wrote later on December 20th, 1729 stating the opera *Lotario* was "too good for the vile taste of the town" and the public in general "love nothing but minuets and ballads, in short the *Beggar's Opera* and *Hurlothrumbo* are only worthy of applause."[173]

Subsequently, Handel's arrangement of pre-existing music by other composers for the production of *Ormisda* had also failed to please:

Mrs. Pendarves to her Sister, Ann Granville

Pall Mall, 4th April 1730.

Operas are dying, to my great mortification. Yesterday I was at the rehearsal of a new one; it is composed of several songs out of Italian operas; but it is very heavy to Mr. Handel's.[174]

---

[172] Ibid.
[173] Ibid. p. 250.
[174] Ibid. p. 254.

Rolli to Riva in Vienna (Translated)

London, 12th June, 1730.

I shall barely answer you on the matter of that *Coppia Eidegrendeliana* [Heidegger-Handel pair] and their worthless operas. Because in truth they succeed no better than they deserve. The musicians will be paid, and that is all can be done. I perceive besides that either there will be no operas in the new season or there will be the same Company, which is certainly going from bad to worse. {...}[175]

When Handel did not have absolute control in the Royal Academy, his operas were evidently more successful. Ironically, now that he had obtained the authority he apparently had campaigned relentlessly to achieve, his first decisions were proving disastrous. These series of events are curious indeed; it is possible this development eventually marred the perception of Handel's ability to manage the production of opera in the eyes of his patrons. Apparently, the greater freedoms granted to Handel did not produce the satisfactory results they expected; eventually the directors would once again support the Italian clique subsequent to a series of misjudgments by Handel, which they vehemently opposed. We shall return to this subject of Handel's managerial errors shortly.

Concurrently, movements towards developing an English style were progressing; Italian opera production became increasingly strained as a result, and once more, Handel's position was situated between the two movements. Scholars have often commented on Handel's "blindness" to the telltale signs that were evident

---

[175] Ibid. pp. 254–255.

concerning the growing popularity for oratorios. We have noticed he only responded and recognised the oratorio genre when ventures such as Lampe and Arne's English opera company were literally pirating his works from the Cannons period. Occasionally, he would compose English works if specifically requested to do so, for example, when Princess Anne requested the composition of the oratorio *Esther*. Apparently, obligatory circumstances motivated Handel rather than artistic freedom. As a result, many scholars conclude that Handel stubbornly resumed his work with Italian opera in defiance and refused to abandon a cherished genre that had become a major part of his life despite the success of these new English projects.

Why would Handel display this obstinate streak as frequently suggested? Dean pointed out that pictorial imagery was a prominent feature of Handel's musical style; Handel also copied in detail scenes and stage directions into his autograph scores.[176] The lack of staged action and scenery in oratorios could have proved a deterrent for Handel; possibly this is one of the reasons for his apparent reluctance concerning English oratorio. However, there is evidence Handel reverted to Italian opera when Bononcini again threatened his position. In addition, Handel's first public attempts with English genres may have been a defensive tactic to protect and maintain his dominant position at the Haymarket in defiance to the pirate companies.

The Demand for English Opera and Handel's Reaction

The resurgence in interest for English opera occurred as the Royal Academy was approaching the breaking point. In the season of 1726–27, Bononcini's *Camilla* was revived at Lincoln's-Inn-Fields

---

[176] Winton Dean, 'Production Style in Handel's Operas,' from *The Cambridge Companion to Handel*, ed. Donald Burrows, (Cambridge University Press, 1997), p. 252.

and had many performances.[177]   Ballad operas too had become increasingly popular after *The Beggar's Opera* in 1728. As Italian opera re-entered a period of instability during the Second Academy, English opera production could be resumed with a greater opportunity for success; therefore we observe ballad operas were augmented by several productions of serious English operas in the Italian style by Lampe and Arne in 1732–33.[178]

Importantly, oratorio was gradually introduced as an English genre during this period when the Philharmonic Society organised a private performance of Handel's *Esther* at the Crown and Anchor Tavern from February 23rd to March 3rd 1732.[179]   According to Deutsch, Handel may have attended the first night of *Esther* for his forty-seventh birthday.[180]   This concert did not attract Handel's attention concerning the possibilities of oratorio until later; it was a private undertaking rather than a public subscription venture and apparently dismissed by him as a one-time occasion. In addition, before this version of *Esther*, Handel's new opera *Sosarme* was successfully produced on 15th of February 1732, and this may have reinforced his interest in Italian opera.[181]   In fact, Handel remained indifferent to *Esther* until approached by Princess Anne; according to Hogwood, the Princess requested Handel to have *Esther* produced, complete with action, at the Haymarket.[182]   However, a pirate version of Handel's work was produced in advance of these plans:

---

[177]   Judith Milhous and Robert D. Hume, 'J.F. Lampe and English Opera at the Little Haymarket in 1732–33,' *Music and Letters*, vol. 78, No. 4 (November, 1997): p. 505.

[178]   See the article by Milhouse and Hume above for a more in depth account of the Lampe and Arne opera productions.

[179]   Deutsch, p. 285.

[180]   Ibid.

[181]   See Viscount Percival's diary entry for February 22nd, 1732 in Deutsch.

[182]   Hogwood, *Handel*, p. 97.

From the "Daily Journal", 19th April 1732

Never Perform'd in Publick before,

At the Great Room in Villars-street York Buildings, To-morrow, being Thursday the 20th of this Instant April, will be perform'd, ESTHER an ORATORIO *or,* Sacred Drama. As it was compos'd originally for the most noble James Duke of Chandos, the Words by Mr. *Pope,* and the Musick by Mr. *Handel.* {...}[183]

Handel reacted immediately to confound the rival performance, for stated in the *Daily Courant* on the same date we find:

By His MAJESTY'S Command

At the King's theatre in the Hay-Market, on Tuesday the 2d Day of May, will be performed, *The Sacred Story* of ESTHER: an *Oratorio* in *English.* Formerly composed by Mr. *Handel,* and now revised by him, with several Additions, and to be performed by a great Number of the best Voices and Instruments.

N.B. There will be no Action on the Stage, but the House will be fitted up in a decent Manner, for the Audience. The Musick to be disposed after the Manner of the Coronation service. {...}[184*]

---

[183] Deutsch, p. 288.
[184] Ibid. pp. 288–289.
* According to Burney, Princess Anne's request for scenery appears to

This was not the only occasion whereupon Handel was compelled to take action regarding English oratorio and opera; before the run of *Esther* was completed, Lampe and Arne pirated his *Acis and Galatea*, in response, Handel immediately revised *Acis and Galatea* with English and Italian text to attract audiences from the various factions supporting English and Italian opera.[185] Handel's revision of *Acis and Galatea* was described as a serenata in the *Daily Courant* and performed on June 10th, 1732.[186]

Interestingly, after the performance of Handel's "Serenata", Bononcini announced that he had arranged to produce a serenata at the same opera house and desired the singer Anna Maria Strada to perform.[187] Bononcini's work was performed as a pastoral entertainment at the end of the season on June 24th, 1732 at the command of Queen Caroline who was acting as regent. It is surprising this incident has not been previously linked with Handel's reluctance to experiment with English genres; Handel resumed opera composition and would not return to oratorios until March 1733 with the premiere of *Deborah*. Handel may have viewed Bononcini's plan to produce his serenata a transgression contrary to his position within the new Academy as he had been granted the authority to elect the composers who would work with him at the Haymarket. Evidently, a rumour circulated Bononcini would become master of his own opera company funded by the Duchess of Marlborough, (a speculation that preceded any plans for the Opera of the Nobility company).[188] In an anonymous pamphlet entitled

---

have been overruled by the bishop of London, Dr. Gibson, who would not permit the use of action with a sacred story in a theatre. Hogwood, *Handel*, p. 98.

[185] Hogwood, *Handel*, p. 99.

[186] Deutsch, p. 294.

[187] Ibid.

[188] See the article 'J.F. Lampe and English Opera' by Milhous and Hume, p. 518.

See and Seem Blind: Or a Critical Dissertation on the Publick Diversions, &c, the author stated he had been:

> {...} inform'd by her Grace the D[uche]ss of M[arlboroug]h, has advance'd very largely towards a new Subscription for Italian Opera's, to be there [Lincolin's Inn Fields] under the direction of Bononcini and Arrigoni; and a new set of Singers, are to be sent for from Italy, for that purpose, {...}[189]

Although this rumour stated Bononcini would occupy Lincolin's-Inn, the fact he usurped the Haymarket for his serenata could imply occupation of the Haymarket remained a possibility for this proposed company. Handel primarily reacted to English performances that were pirate productions of his own works, and he returned to Italian opera around the time of Bononcini's interference, suggesting Handel was resuming his defensive stratagem concerning his right of control and authoritative position at the Haymarket.

Handel also ignored other productions of English opera following Bononcini's serenata, including the operas his student John Christopher Smith was involved with, such as *Teraminta* and *Ulysses*.[190] Astonishingly, Handel apparently set aside Aaron Hill's famous letter of December 5th, 1732 pleading with him to "deliver us from our Italian bondage."[191]

Therefore, the previous observation that Handel was initially blind and deaf to the English cause may be credible to a point. However, is it possible he reverted to Italian opera when an old rival

---

[189] From *See and Seem Blind: Or a Critical Dissertation on the Publick Diversions, &c,* (London: 1732), in Milhous and Hume, 'J.F. Lampe and English Opera,' p. 518.

[190] Hogwood, *Handel,* p. 99. See also William C. Smith, 'More Handeliana,' *Music and Letters,* vol XXXIV no. 1 (January, 1953): p. 13.

[191] Deutsch, p. 209.

from Rolli's circle threatened his authority at the Haymarket? This possibility has not been previously suggested as far as I am aware, and I would like to propose this as a new theory. If this hypothetical situation is examined and considered with the series of events that occurred in the two years previous to Handel's relocation to Covent Garden, the conditions set forth in the contract between Heidegger and Handel might be clarified. The importance regarding the nature of this contract may have a direct bearing on when and why they both separated, concluding with Handel's move to Covent Garden. We will now attempt to examine this contract in the next section.

Handel's Rebellion and His Contract with Heidegger

When Bononcini was granted permission to re-enter the opera house for the production of his serenata, theoretically without Handel's full consent, Handel may have concluded that his patrons had reneged on their part of the agreement with him and Heidegger. It had been previously agreed that as head composer Handel could elect those with whom he preferred to work. However, by Royal command, and perhaps with more encouragement from his supporters, Bononcini was permitted to have his serenata produced after Handel's serenata of *Acis and Galatea*, which could be construed as a competitive move. Finally, Handel took matters into his own hands and rebelled — justified in his conviction that the patrons were in breech of their agreement.

One strikingly seditious incident on Handel's part is evident with his production of *Deborah* in March 1733. When Handel eventually returned to oratorio composition, he decided on a drastic course of action that infuriated all his subscription holders including the underwriters of the Second Academy. He raised the ticket prices to one guinea, encouraged by Princess Anne, and refused the subscribers the use of their silver tickets previously issued to members of the Second Academy.[192] This incited an uproar when the subscribers forced entry into the theatre and demanded their privilege. One may assume Handel raised the prices to cover the cost of the enlarged orchestra and the addition of the chorus, and this may have been a contributing factor. However, Handel's actions also raises other observations; apparently, he did not announce that prices would have to be raised to cover these extra expenses, and one would expect the courtesy of a public announcement. The fact he refused the Academy subscribers highlights important clues concerning this new development.

This oratorio production was possible perceived by Handel as a separate venture from his opera productions as he excluded the subscribers who had hired Heidegger when the opera venture was re-established to arrange the house rents and manage the theatre. By arranging ticket sales, etc., Handel was effectively overriding Heidegger's authority, or maybe Heidegger stepped aside, suggesting Handel was assuming full responsibility for this oratorio venture.

Immediately Handel was ridiculed in an article printed in the *Craftsman* on April 7th, 1733 due to this outrage caused by the ticket scandal. (See Appendix Five.) It has been previously accepted the attack was primarily directed at the current Prime Minister Robert Walpole with regard to his infamous Tobacco Excise Bill; yet, we cannot overlook the fact that it was printed with reference to Handel. Two contentious issues were simultaneously addressed, and if we review this article with these two associations in reverse, i.e. it was primarily an attack on Handel with reference to Walpole, we are presented with an extraordinary scenario offering a unique perspective of the Second Academy.

First, Handel's significant authority was ridiculed and his management of the operas was criticised. Handel was very selective concerning his choice of singers and his method in assigning their

---

[192] Ibid. pp. 309–310.

roles was also rebuked. Apparently, the public was dissatisfied with his management, resulting with a decrease in attendance at his productions. Handel's productions with Heidegger were initially unsuccessful, as we observed earlier; therefore this section of the article corresponds with the events that had occurred. Interestingly, he was accused of proclaiming, "there was no Composer in England but Himself" — if Handel had opposed Bononcini returning to the Haymarket, this criticism also had logical connections with these current events.

Second, there is a peculiar accusation that Handel formulated a plan "to establish his Power and Fortune by Force." Of particular interest to us is the statement, "at a proper Season" he would declare his intentions to the public, and this "plan" would be accomplished for the "Advantage" of everyone, "and his *Opera's* in particular." It seems Handel had envisioned a special project concerning one of the opera seasons; we will examine this point later.

Third, the article mentions a "Brother" who agreed with his programme, and Handel, with the "Advice of *his Brother*, at last produces his *Project*" — this must signify Heidegger who was Handel's partner.

Next, there is an accusation that the patrons would not share in the profits of this "plan". It is mentioned in the article Handel had called the subscribers a "Parcel of Rogues," and proceeded to stop certain "Abuses" occurring which he pointed out as the cause of the "Decay of {the} *Opera's*" due to their (the patrons'?) "Cheapness."

Finally, the oratorio of *Deborah* is proclaimed as the "Plan." The article relates that Handel had assumed all aspects of the management, including the selling of the tickets by "Officers of his own naming." The most important point to observe, Handel was accused of scheming to "pocket" all the profits from the oratorio based upon the notion "the very being of Opera's depended upon him singly" and the whole production would be for "his *own Benefit.*"

I suggest this article substantiates the theory that Handel's intention was to assume control of the opera venture completely for the remainder of his term with Heidegger, and calculated he could support it by producing oratorios. Handel would finally eliminate his "untrustworthy" patrons whom he believed failed to honour their agreement. This theory may seem preposterous, but it can be supported with further documentation recording subsequent events.

Handel's drastic decision to dismiss Senesino at the end of the 1732–33 season in May of 1733 supports this theory. Apparently, Handel had not notified the subscribers of this sudden change in casting which was quite unexpected:

From the "Bee", 2nd June 1733

We are credibly informed, that one Day last Week Mr. *H–d–l*, Director-General of the Opera-House, sent a Message to Signior *Senesino*, the famous *Italian Singer*, acquainting Him, that He had no further Occasion for his Service: and that *Senesino* replied, the next Day, by a Letter, containing a full Resignation of all his Parts in the *Opera*, which He had performed for many Years with great Applause — We hope the polite Mr. *Washingham* will give us Leave to observe, upon this Occasion, that the *World seems greatly ASTONISH'D at so unexpected an Event; and that all true lovers of Musick GRIEVE to see so fine a singer dismissed, in so critical a Conjuncture.*[193]

Recently, new information concerning the dismissal of Senesino has surfaced; it had been assumed and generally accepted Handel fired Senesino when he realised the performer was involved with the plans for the new Opera of the Nobility company, which supposedly had been organised in January of 1733 without his

---

[193] Ibid. pp. 315–316.

knowledge. It had been theorised that Handel, upon discovering this clandestine project, was furious with Senesino's seeming disloyalty and fired him as a result, whereupon Senesino publicly defected to the Opera of the Nobility. However, the new information recently uncovered suggests this sequence of events was not the cause of Senesino's dismissal.

Thomas McGeary discovered in 1998 that Deutsch misdated the well-known letter by John West, Baron De la Warr to the Duke of Richmond as from January 1733; it is in fact dated *June the 16th, 1733*:

June the 16: 1733.

[...] There is A Spirit got up against the Dominion of Mr. Handel, A Subscription carry'd on, and Directors chosen, who have contracted with Senesino, and have sent for Cuzzoni, and Farinelli. It is hoped he will come as soon as the Carneval of Venice is over, if not sooner. The General Court gave power to contract with any Singer Except Strada, So that it is Thought Handel must fling up, which the Poor Count [Heidegger] will not be sorry for, There being no one but what declares as much for him, as against the Other [Handel], so that we have a good Chance of Seeing Operas once more on a good foot. Porpora is sent for. {...}The Directrs. chosen are as follows. D. of Bedford, Lds. Bathurst, Burlington, Cowper, Limmerick, Stair, Lovel, Cadogan, DeLawarr, & D. of Rutland. Sr John Buckworth. Henry Furnese Esq. Sr Micl. Newton;* There seems great Unanimity, and Resolution to carry on the Undertaking comme il faut.[194]

---

* Notice that the list of directors includes many of Rolli's patrons.
[194] West Sussex Record Office. Goodwood MS 103, f. 173–75, in Thomas McGeary, 'Handel, Prince Frederick, and the Opera of the

This new information is very important as we can now date the *first known reference* concerning the formation of the Opera of the Nobility to June 13th, 1733 by a notice printed in the *Daily Post*:

> The Subscribers to the Opera in which Signor Senesino and Signora Cuzzoni are to perform, are desired to meet at Mr. Hickford's Great Room in Panton-street, on Friday next [the 15th] by Eleven o'Clock, in order to settle proper Methods for carrying on the Subscription. {…}[195]

Therefore, as De la Warr's letter is dated June 16th, we observe he was recounting the decisions reached during this meeting held in Mr. Hickford's Great Room on June 15th.

Supremely important, Handel did not fire Senesino on grounds of disloyalty — the Opera of the Nobility *was not planned until after Handel had unexpectedly dismissed Senesino in the latter part of May.* Apparently, Handel acted on his own initiative; this was an unwise decision regarding a singer the patrons admired, suggesting he was determined to manage the company without their support, and is similar to his decision to act as impresario for the production of *Deborah*. The *Craftsman* article featuring the "Handel/Walpole" controversy previously reported Handel appointed himself responsible for the operas. This would explain the inference in the article with the announcement; "at a proper Season" he would declare his intentions to the public, and that this "plan" would be an "Advantage" for everyone, "and his *Opera's* in particular."

Would Bononcini's interference at the Haymarket force Handel into this course of action, and is there additional proof

---

Nobility Reconsidered,' *Göttinger Händel-Beiträge* 7 (1998): p. 157.
[195]   Deutsch, p. 316.

Handel assumed control of the company as a result?

First, Strada had refused to sing in Bononcini's serenata as requested. There is an article in the *Craftsman* that reported Strada's husband insisted she refuse Bononcini's offer; this same article also related the resumption of the rivalry between Handel, Bononcini, and their supporters at the performance of the serenata:

From the "Craftsman" 12th August 1732

[Anonymous letter to the editor]

> ... This brought me up, last Week, upon a Friend's having written me Word that some Musick of Bononcini was to be perform'd at the *Opera House*, of which He knew I was a great Admirer; but being very much disappointed at the Performance, I went afterwards to pass the Evening with some of my Acquaintance, who were Lovers of *Musick* as well as my self, in order to get some Information about it ... several Stories were told for and against the *two late famous Antagonists* ... At last, one of the Company had Curiosity to ask what might have been the Occasion that the *Serenata* was not continued; to which another made Answer that it fell out chiefly by the means of *Strada's Husband*, who would not suffer his Wife to sing in it; {...}[196]

The fact the nobility refused to consider Strada for their new company, as stated by De la Warr's letter of June 16th, suggests they were incensed with her refusal to perform in Bononcini's serenata in accordance with her husband's wishes. This implies the nobility sympathised with Bononcini, indicating that their quarrel with

---

[196] Ibid. p. 295.

Handel included this incident and did not rest solely with the dismissal of Senesino. In addition, according to the "Handel/Walpole" article, they suspected Strada of supporting Handel with his "plan" concerning *Deborah* and the usurpation of the company; these two incidents may explain why Strada remained faithful to Handel while the other singers defected to the Opera of the Nobility company.

Senesino's dismissal may have resulted from the Bononcini "threat". Handel and Senesino were continually in conflict as we have noted; as Handel was assuming responsibility for the operas, he may have calculated the advantage of hiring singers who were amicable. In addition, Senesino was expensive to retain in the company; when he returned to London for the Second Academy, his salary was finally agreed with the directors at 1,400 pounds instead of the proposed 1,200 pounds.[197] If Handel intended to take charge of the company, it is conceivable he considered eliminating expenses where possible. It was this decision, including the "*Deborah* incident" that outraged the nobility who subsequently adopted Senesino as their "mascot" to rally additional support for their new company. We note Senesino's name was included in the lease for the Lincoln's-Inn-Fields theatre.[198] In fact, the nobility and the former directors were so disgusted by Handel's actions at this point the first article in the foundation contract of the new company stated: "Point d'accommodement à jamais avec le Sr Händel."[199]

The possibility that Handel assumed control of the Second Academy is also evident in the nature of Heidegger and Handel's partnership. There are several theories that attempt to explain the

---

[197] Compare Owen Swiney's and Handel's letters. Deutsch, pp. 258, 261.

[198] Dorris, *Italian Circle*, p. 114.

[199] My closest translations; "To never be accommodating with Sr Handel," or "Not to be accommodating, and never with Sr. Handel." See the *Dispatch Addressed to Caspar Wilhelm von Brocke*, January 1734 in Deutsch, p. 341.

conditions set forth in their contract, and if we endeavour to interpret these various accounts, the possibility that Handel was free to act in this manner may be established.

The first major clue may be found in Mainwaring's version. Mainwaring claimed their contract stipulated a partnership comprising of three years whereby they would subsist from year to year. Mainwaring also stated Handel "ventured to continue Operas at the Haymarket for one year on his own bottom."[200] This is an interesting statement as this indicates a four-year term. Importantly, he mentions that despite the formation of the rival Opera of the Nobility company, *Handel decided to manage on his own for one year*:

> {...} for about the time of the separation at the Hay-market, occasioned by the disagreement between HANDEL and his Singers, many of the Nobility raised a new subscription in order to carry on another Opera at Lincoln's-inn fields, in which they could have Singers and Composers of their own chusing. [sic.] {...} Tho' HANDEL bore up against this opposition, he soon felt the effects of it; and yet, *at the expiration* of the three years partnership with HEIDEGGER, he ventured to continue Operas at the Hay-market for one year on his own bottom.[201]

If we consider this particular account, Handel decided to manage the Haymarket company personally for one year — the same year the Opera of the Nobility was founded. However, Handel and Heidegger remained at the Haymarket for five years, and Mainwaring misplaced a year in his calculation; this may be due to the fact he was relying on anecdotes, and it would not be too

---

[200] Mainwaring, p. 115.
[201] Ibid. pp. 113–115.

difficult to have certain dates and facts confused under these circumstances. However, evidence of the fifth year still exists in his account.

After the supposed four years, Mainwaring mentions Handel relocated to Lincoln's-Inn-Fields when the rival company vacated.[202] This statement we know is not factual. Subsequently, Mainwaring confuses where *Arianna in Creta* was produced, and the actual location of the Opera of the Nobility:

> In the summer of the year 1733, he made a tour to Oxford, {...} The next winter his Opera of ARIANNA was performed at Covent Garden, while another was performed of the same name, composed by PORPORA, was acted in the Hay-market.[203]

In fact, Handel was at the King's Theatre in the Haymarket with the production of *Arianna*, at the exact time, the Opera of the Nobility company was present at Lincoln's-Inn. However, the venues could be correct if we attempt to establish which season he is referring to.

His account implies the season of 1733–34 or 1734–35 as the "next winter" could signify that forthcoming winter, or the winter after 1733. If he implied the 1733–34 season, the places are incorrect although the opera productions are exact. If he is suggesting the 1734–35 season, then the places are accurate, but the production times are miscalculated by one year; when Mainwaring cannot provide a concluding date for Handel's term at Covent Garden, he simply states:

> At the end of three or four years {at Covent Garden}, instead of having acquired such an addition to

---

202 Ibid.
203 Ibid. p. 119.

his fortune, as from his care, industry, and abilities, he had reason to expect, he was obliged to draw out of the funds almost all that he was worth, in order to answer the demands upon him.[204]

Seemingly Mainwaring was unable to compute the information he received concerning the four year contract; he leaves the final date open for speculation as one year is not accounted for according to the events, and this also explains his confusion with the venues.

In other accounts, the five-year nature of the contract is maintained; this in part originates from the permit granted to Handel and Heidegger for their use of the Academy's equipment for five years. The Earl of Shaftsbury wrote in 1760 that their partnership existed for five years.[205] Hawkins maintains Mainwaring's account of three years, with one additional year where Handel managed by himself.[206] Burney states that Handel initiated the engagement with Heidegger, who was in possession of the house, and agreed the management would be carried at their own risk.[207]

Scholars have strived to interpret these sources and presented different theories. Streatfeild maintained Handel had complete charge of the Second Academy and simply rented the theatre from

---

[204] Ibid. pp. 120–121.

[205] Quoted from Deutsch in Robert D. Hume, 'Handel and Opera Management in London in the 1730s,' *Music and Letters*, vol. 67 no. 4 (October, 1986): p. 349.

[206] From Sir John Hawkins, *A General History of the Science and Practice of Music (1776)* 3nd edn., London, 1853 (reprinted New York, 1963), ii. 976, in 'Handel and Opera Management,' ibid.

[207] From Charles Burney, *A General History of Music (1776–89)* ed. Frank Mercer, London, 1935 (reprinted New York, 1957), ii 760 in 'Handel and Opera Management,' ibid.

Heidegger.[208]   He asserted that Heidegger dropped Handel and rented out the Haymarket to the Opera of the Nobility when the lease on the theatre expired in July of 1734.[209]   Paul Henry Lang proposed that in 1729 Heidegger and Handel planned to continue on their own funded by their private resources.[210]   Hogwood stated they did not enter into an actual partnership and their contract terminated in the spring of 1734.[211]

So, what are the possibilities? The three-year venture does not compute as they actually remained at the Haymarket for the full five years. However, the concept that Handel decided to carry the risks for one year is possible according to the re-examination of documentary evidence presented above, i.e. the "Handel/Walpole" article and the interpretations of Mainwaring and Hawkins. Hence, I would like to offer a new theory on the nature of their contract.

Initially, Handel and Heidegger may have agreed upon a three-year venture that would subsist from year to year. They presented their proposals to the directors for approval, however, the directors decided to allow them a longer term with the company stock; perhaps the directors were more optimistic with this venture. Handel and Heidegger may then have decided to extend their original plan to five years, and to subsist from year to year according to their original agreement. The possibility they could still "subsist" remains as the five years allocated by the directors was for free use of the Academy equipment and was not for a formal business contract with them as such.

In the fourth season, Handel possibly arrived at the conclusion the nobility had broken their agreement by allowing Bononcini to produce his serenata when they had bestowed upon

---

[208]   From R. A. Streatfeild, Handel, London, (1909), p. 118 in 'Handel and Opera Manadement,' ibid.

[209]   Ibid.

[210]   From Paul Henry Lang, *George Frideric Handel* (New York: 1966), p. 234, in 'Handel and Opera Management,' f. 10, ibid.

[211]   Hogwood, *Handel*, p. 123.

him absolute control over the management of the music sector of the productions. Apparently, Handel devised a plan to support the next season by producing concerts and other performances, and thereby unchain himself from his dependency upon the patrons, which explains why he raised ticket prices for *Deborah* and refused the subscription tickets. Moreover, the "Handel/Walpole" article states that Handel, acting in the best interests of his operas, appointed himself solely responsible for them.

At first, Heidegger, Handel's "Brother" in the article, seems to be supportive of this autocratic decision. It has been suggested that although the operas were financially unstable, Handel and Heidegger could have continued production indefinitely supported by the proceeds from Heidegger's masked balls and Handel's lucrative concerts at Oxford in 1733,[212] and this may have evolved into Handel's concert programme. In contemporary documents dating from the nineteenth and the twenty-first of July 1733, it was reported Handel earned 2000 pounds or more at Oxford.[213] Handel was invited to Oxford due to the revival of the "Publick Act";[214] he may have viewed this invitation as an opportunity to support his project due to the forthcoming concerts. This could also explain why Handel did not receive his honorary Doctorate; he explained later in 1744, "I neither could nor would accept the Doctor's degree, because I was overwhelmingly busy."[215] This remark implies Handel was preoccupied with his concerts at Oxford and went there for the

---

[212]   See Judith Milhous and Robert D. Hume, 'Handel's Opera Finances in 1732–33,' *Musical Times*, 125 (1984): p. 89.

[213]   Deutsch, p. 328.

[214]   The Act, an elaborate degree-conferring ceremony held in the Sheldonian Theatre, was revived by the Vice Chancellor of Oxford University, Dr. William Holmes, who invited Handel to take part. See Deutsch p. 316, and Hogwood, *Handel*, p. 107.

[215]   From a letter which is now lost, a fragment of it is quoted in L. C. Mizler, *Neu eröffnete Musikalische Bibliothek* (Leipzig, 1736-54), in Hogwood, *Handel*, p. 117.

sole purpose of supporting his opera-plan at the Haymarket.

However, we may observe his greatest folly was in dismissing Senesino. Handel, ensconced as self-appointed manager of his operas — liberated from the authority of the directors and subscribers — now had the opportunity of acquiring the singers of his choice and would eliminate additional expenses arising from Senesino's salary. Heidegger may have been alarmed by Handel's unorthodox actions and decided to avoid investing his profits with his project, which explains why Handel decided to manage one year "on his own bottom." A document exists supporting this theory — a manuscript with an accounting of the income for the 1732–33 opera season.[216] The most important section is contained in the second part where Strada's salary has been tallied, including an accounting for all the arrears "remaining due to ye 2 Undertakers for ye 1st 2d 3d & 4th seasons." (See Appendix Six.) What is this document actually suggesting?

This accounting evidently displays a finalization of the business agreement for the first four years of their venture. Judith Milhous and Robert Hume observed no apparent reason why Strada's account would be tallied at that point, including the arrears for these four seasons, (unless the managers, startled by the low rate of income, wanted to compare each season).[217] It is important to note the term "ye 2 Undertakers"; apparently, Handel and Heidegger's agreement is still in effect at this time as they are referred to as two joint managers or partners. It is unusual the accounts should be examined at this time in their venture, suggesting circumstances had changed and Handel planned to support the last year while Heidegger decided to withdraw. This freedom to change their plans remained a possibility if they decided to comply with the "subsist from year to year" programme, and explains why Heidegger subsequently leased his theatre to the Opera of the Nobility.

---

[216] Milhous and Hume, 'Handel's Opera Finances,' pp. 86–89.

[217] Ibid. p. 88.

Heidegger did not participate in Handel's operatic venture for the last season, and when the Academy permit expired, he had the option to rent his theatre to the financially secure company currently funded by the nobility. I conclude, Handel and Heidegger's initial three-year agreement could have been extended to five years whereby they engaged to subsist from year to year, with Handel deciding to continue solely that last year without financial support from Heidegger.

One question remains to be answered concerning the formation of the Nobility Opera; what prompted the directors to form their new company before Handel's contract had concluded? Handel would have been forced to vacate the Haymarket, as the Academy's permit would eventually expire. However, it is a fact Senesino returned abruptly to Italy when the Royal Academy collapsed; he may not have waited for Handel's contract to expire, therefore the nobility may have formed the new company to entice him to remain in England. This would also explain their synonymous use of his name with the new company as it was stamped on everything from the lease to the tickets in an attempt to placate him, which is evident in a letter printed in *The Old Whig* on March 20th 1735:

> ... The late Squabble at the Opera is pretty well adjusted. It had rose very high; Parties were formed, and Protests were just ready to be enter'd, to which many fair Hands had threaten'd to subscribe; when by accomodating Matters with Senesino, all the ruffled Passions were calmed, as it had been by the Melody of his Voice. {...}[218]

Ironically, while Handel may have been defending his position within the Second Academy from Rolli's supporters, he had

---

[218] Deutsch, p. 384.

exasperated the existing tensions with his patrons and thereby facilitated the formation of the Opera of the Nobility company. The nobility had granted Handel signal authority in the Second Academy in an attempt to solve the problems created earlier in the Royal Academy. At first, this was proving unsuccessful, and the nobility may have concluded they had made an inexplicable error in judgement. In addition, the Italians were not satisfied with the directors' arrangements with Handel, and he supplied them with the excuse to revolt against his management with the *Deborah* incident and his drastic expulsion of Senesino. Naturally, the nobility and the directors were infuriated with Handel's appropriation of the venture by hypocritically appointing himself impresario when he had previously refused this position offered to him in 1728. Therefore, the nobility supported by the Italians retaliated to his actions. In fact, Rolli may have written the "Handel/Walpole" article criticising Handel's decisions.

Deutsch maintains Rolli never displayed his antagonism for Handel in public despite his animosity towards him, and therefore states the article could have been written by one of Rolli's associates who intended to highlight their past skirmishes.[219] However, Dorris presented a credible argument that Rolli did indeed compose the article based upon his study of the letters Rolli had written to Senesino, comparing it with Rolli's translation style.[220] The fact Rolli had lost his position as Italian Secretary at the Royal Academy in consequence of Walpole's administration supplies him with a strong motive to satirise Walpole and explains the dual implications in the article. (See f. 113.) Finally, when Handel dismissed Senesino, he provided the nobility with a motive to re-establish; united with the Italians, they formed the Opera of the Nobility in opposition to Handel.

---

[219] Milhous and Hume, 'Handel's Opera Finances,' p. 312–313

[220] Dorris, *Italian Circle*, pp. 103–112. His source; the letter "Al Sigr. Calebi d'Anvrsa" among the Senesino papers in the Biblioteca Comunale in Siena.

In the interim, opera entered an evolutionary phase resulting from these new struggles; whereas Italian operas were once composed primarily within the heroic vein, works produced during this period were now reflecting pastoral elements. Apparently, the Arcadian-influenced Italians had contributed to this new development, however its foundations were deeply entrenched with the resurgence in the demand for English opera.

A Change in Production and Musical Style
During the Second Academy

During this transition period from Italian opera to English oratorio after the fall of the Royal Academy, Handel progressed by combining both styles reflecting these trends; he was generally observant when styles were changing and was open to experimentation. When examining the structure of his operas dating from his first public English productions in 1732, it is apparent there was an effort on Handel's part to compose works that would encompass all the various reforms occurring. Handel apparently strived to placate both factions while remaining true to his quest for artistic freedom and his ambition to retain his position of authority.

At this time, pastoral forms gradually replaced the heroic operas of the Royal Academy days.[221] Ironically, the return of the pastoral style may have reawakened the rivalry between Handel and the Italians, commencing with the introduction of the English production of *Acis and Galetea*. Interestingly, Harris mentions scholars have failed to explain why Bononcini would produce a

---

[221] Harris, *Pastoral Tradition*, pp. 210–211. Harris mentions that Handel had continued with his heroic style of composing while managing the Haymarket Theatre with Heidegger until he produced *Acis and Galetea*.

pastoral in June 1732.[222] If we consider Rolli's Italian circle in London, so closely related to the Arcadians who were keenly involved with opera reforms centring on pastoral conventions, and link this association with the circle's disappointment at Bononcini's exclusion from the new venture, Bononcini's introduction of a pastoral may not be as enigmatic as one might expect. The members of the circle, disgruntled with Handel's newly gained authority as noted previously, were proved correct in their doubts concerning his managerial capabilities when his first productions were not very successful. When the pastoral concept was suddenly reintroduced successfully by English composers, particularly by Handel, when it had failed in the earlier part of the century in London, this change in public appreciation of opera may have signalled the occasion to regain their control. This may have presented the opportunity they anticipated; as the pastoral gained popularity in England, the Arcadians could promote reformed Italian opera, and Bononcini's work may have been the catalyst for them in this purpose. If this theory is acceptable, it may explain Handel's sudden and drastic plan to personally manage the venture before the Italians could return to the Haymarket, thereby preventing a repetition of the Royal Academy debacle. Interestingly, Handel continued to compose in the pastoral vein according to Harris until 1736.[223]

Handel composed *Orlando* (1733) before Senesino's dismissal, and this was his first return to opera in the pastoral style after nineteen productions of heroic operas.[224] According to Dean, it is also classed as a magic opera;[225] Handel only composed five magic operas, three are prior to the Royal Academy, *Rinaldo* (1711), *Teseo* (1713), and *Amadigi* (1715), years later he composed *Orlando* (1733), and for his first Covent Garden period,

---

[222] Ibid. p. 224.

[223] Ibid. p. 211.

[224] Ibid. p. 225.

[225] Harris, *Pastoral Tradition*, p. 225, quoting from Dean, *Opera Seria*.

Alcina (1735). We have observed the Arcadians were disinterested in scenery and magic-operas; perhaps this paucity of magic orientated operas during the Royal Academy reflects the influence they had regarding the productions during that period. Now that Handel was planning to operate the Second Academy, commencing with his last year with Heidegger, his creativity was no longer restricted by their influence in this area and he could now return to the form of operas that were particularly successful for him when he first arrived in England.

Obviously, an anglicized Italian version was preferred, with spectacular scenery; subsequently, the pastoral was merging with one of the conventions the English favoured. Handel's early magic operas provided an avenue for these productions, and we may observe history repeating; Handel resumed the anglicization process, and was successful with *Orlando*. The pastoral was not rejected as in the past; hence, the development of opera would continue in this direction, particularly after the formation of the Italian Opera of the Nobility company. Competition was rife — the Opera of the Nobility produced their stylized pastoral opera *Arianna in Naxos* following Handel's *Arianna in Creta* in 1734, and they also produced their own opera based on the Acis and Galatea myth called *Polifemo* for the 1734–35 season.

Operas were zealously produced in a competitive atmosphere as the rival companies vied for support from the public; the Italians now had their own company in which they could produce their operas according to their ideology. Handel's actions regarding the management of *Deborah* and Senesino's dismissal were unfortunate as this encouraged his patrons to support the opposition, and momentarily, the Italians had triumphed over Handel; Rolli believed the Opera of the Nobility signalled the beginning of "better days" for him as he was now employed as librettist.[226] Certain members of the nobility concluded they would finally be presented with operas

---

[226] Dorris, *Italian Circle*, p. 154.

produced "on a better foot" as De La Warr's letter of June 1733 points out.

During Handel's last year at the Haymarket, the source librettos for his new works suggest Handel endeavoured with all his power and skill to recapture his audience, and resorted to setting librettos written by the Arcadian masters; two of his new operas are based on texts by Metastasio, and one by Zeno. (See Appendix Four.) This is a significant number of new productions based on Arcadian texts for one season, and is worthy of our attention when we consider Handel's apparent reluctance to work with their librettos. Strohm reinforces the possibility Handel may have been catering to the public's preference that season rather than his ideals as a composer, as he observed Handel continually resisted Metastasio's texts after 1732 notwithstanding Metastasio was perceived as a "European institution."[227]

However, Handel did not comply solely with Italian conventions to encourage audiences to attend his productions; he also experimented with the English demand for the reformation of opera. Ironically, these reforms resembled the conventions that the Arcadians had introduced; the English ideal of reformation may have been propagated by the Italian/Arcadian presence in London from earlier days. One major debate centred on the power of poetry and music as an effective method of teaching virtue, to instruct, and to inspire the noblest of emotions.[228] This corresponds with what *opera seria* was intended to achieve through the application of heroic subjects as an exemplary method to instil virtue. However, the English introduced a variation to this Arcadian plan; they now regarded adaptations of a religious nature more appropriate for this purpose, hence we can appreciate the development of English oratorio in this instance. This was an important national issue, as English church and state were considered almost inseparable; Ruth

---

[227] Strohm, *Italian Essays*, pp. 226–227.
[228] See Chapters One and Two in Smith, *Oratorios*.

Smith relates a moral void was perceived in the theatre and for the health of the nation, this moral deprivation needed to be addressed. [229] The reformers adopted the principles of Greek tragedy as their example, for as Smith states, "It was a public art form instilling consciousness of national history and an aspiration to public service."[230]

Importantly, this national ideal promoted interest in the revival of the chorus; due to this new interest in the application of moral allegory, Athenian tragedy with its convention of the chorus was perceived as the foremost genre that should be imitated in this effort.[231] In a book attributed to James Ralph entitled *The Touch-Stone*: {...} *By a Person of Some Taste and Quality* {...} (1728) this call for reviving the chorus was proclaimed, and the absence of this element within Italian opera in England was criticised:

> A superior Genius ought to preside in the Conduct of these Affairs, lest we be mistaken in the End propos'd and have our Performances turn'd into Ridicule, when we expect they should be admir'd ... In Fine, a CHORUS rightly introduc'd in an OPERA, must give the WORLD the *NE PLUS ULTRA* of MUSICK; and, I think it manifest, that by the wilful and careless Omission of it on the present *Italian Stage*, we lose the Perfection of *Harmony*; and never allow our Composers an Opportunity of exerting their highest Talents, and displaying the Greatness of a Genius, by shewing what Force of MUSICK can produce.
>
> WE may have an Idea of this from some Parts of our CHURCH-MUSICK; which though generally very bad, yet demonstrates, that those full Parts of

---

[229] Ibid. p. 69.
[230] Ibid. p. 56.
[231] Ibid. pp. 60–70.

MUSICK, either in CHURCH or THEATRE, shew the Quintessence of Art in the Composer, and must give equal Delight to an Audience.[232]

Hence we observe the gradual development of chorus in opera similar to that heard in church music, as opposed to the brief *coro* typical in Italian Baroque opera; this element would now emerge as one of the most prominent characteristics of Handel's oratorios and his operas during the mid to late 1730s.

An interesting example may be noted with Handel's inclusion of the chorus in *Acis and Galatea*.[233] Handel composed three terzettos functioning as a form of chorus for the first version performed at Cannons, however, in the second version for the Haymarket, Handel incorporated a standard chorus to introduce nymphs and shepherds. In addition, Handel illustrated a novel concept with the chorus in Act II when it addresses Galatea in *da capo* form:

Galatea, e coro (Act II)

---

[232]   From James Ralph, *The Touch-stone; or Historical, Critical, Political, Philosophical and Theological Essays on the Reigning Diversions of the Town. Design'd for the Improvement of all Authors, Spectators, and Actors of Operas, Plays, and Masquerades. In which Every Thing Antique, or Modern, relating to Musick, Poetry, Dancing, Pantomimes Chorusses, Cat-Calls, Audiences, Judges, Criticks, Balls, Ridottos, Assemblies, New Oratory, Circus, Bear-Garden, Gladiators, Prize-Fighters, Italian Strolers, Mountebank Stages, Cock-Pits, Puppet-Shews, Fairs, and Publick Auctions, is occasionally Handled. By a Person of Some Taste and Quality. With a Preface, giving an Account of the Author and the Work (1728)*; pp. 124 -7, in Smith, pp. 65–66. See also the article by Irving Lowens, 'The Touch-Stone (1729): A Neglected View of London Opera,' *The Musical Quarterly*, 45 (1959): pp. 325–342 concerning this document.

[233]   G. F. Handel, *Aci, Galatea, e Polofemo. Serenata di G. F. Handel*, Kalmus Miniature Score Series, No. 1295 (New York: Edwin F. Kalmus).

Galatea:	Vuoi veder dov' è la calma
	Vuoi trovad'Amor la palma
	Vien-
Coro: Dov' è?	
Galatea:	In questo sen.
	Io mi struggo per diletto
	Si.
Coro: Perche?	
Galatea:	Stampò l'affetto
	Bella imago del mio ben
	Vien-
Coro; Dov' è?	
Galatea:	In questo sen.
Coro: Renda Giove al fido petto	
	Viver lungo e ognor seren.
Galatea:	Vuoi veder: _Da Capo._

In Act II, the chorus is used as a concluding *da capo* sequence "Smiling Venus, Queen of Love." In Act III, the chorus begins a *da capo* sequence "Viver, e non amar," and the chorus is incorporated into the finale, "Galatea, dry thy tears." Handel would continue to utilise a *da capo* format for his future works, structuring chorus into "block" *da capo*-type sequences to create momentum in the finales.

A further example of Handel's use of chorus following the productions of *Acis and Galatea* and oratorios *Deborah* and *Athalia*, is observed in his serenata *Il Parnasso in Festa* performed on March 13th, 1734; there are thirteen brief choral sections, six in Act I, four in Act II, and three in Act III.[234] In addition, the revival of his earlier pastoral *Il Pastor Fido* on May 18th 1734 preceding his move

---

[234] G. F. Handel, *Al Parnasso in Festa; Serenata*, Kalmus Miniature Score Series, No. 1304 (New York: Edwin F. Kalmus).

to Covent Garden also displays his enthusiastic efforts to introduce the concept of chorus into his works:

From the "Daily Journal" 18th May 1734

> At the King's Theatre ... this present Saturday ... will be perform'd, An Opera, call'd PASTOR FIDO. Composed by Mr. HANDEL. Intermixed with Chorus's. The Scenery after a particular Manner ... .[235]

Of paramount importance, Handel previously experimented with the concept of using chorus before he transferred to Covent Garden. This period of Handel's career is striking as he obviously considered the English preference for chorus, and adhered to the pastoral in an attempt to placate the expectations of the Italian opera-preferring public. Evidently, Handel did not require the forces available at Covent Garden to initially inspire his creative ability concerning the use of chorus; however, when he vacated the Haymarket, this change of venue proved advantageous to his operatic development.

---

[235] Deutsch, p. 365.

Chapter 4

Handel at Covent Garden:
The Circumstances Effecting His Relocation

The actual circumstances effecting Handel's relocation to Covent Garden in 1734 have been debated by scholars at length. Was Handel's move an action of necessity, or a decision he made to further his own aims?   One could argue it was primarily out of necessity, which in turn had great advantages for him; also, there are indications that Handel was fully aware of his forthcoming transition.

It has been theorised in the past Handel was simply abandoned by Heidegger in favour of the Opera of the Nobility, and was forced to hastily secure a suitable theatre before the next season commenced. This theory implies Handel was compelled or obliged to use the forces at Covent Garden and was innovative without actually employing his own initiative. This concept had been supported by Dean's observation, resulting from his study of the autograph score, that Handel commenced his first work for Covent Garden, *Ariodante*, for the cast of singers at the Haymarket and not the Covent Garden cast, and thereby he assumed Handel had no knowledge of his forthcoming eviction. [236]   Dean states as further evidence Handel may have been unaware of the availability of the ballet troupe, for he surmised the dances were added between September 9th, and October 24th, while work on Act III continued, thus supporting the notion of Handel's ignorance regarding Heidegger's intentions.[237]

---

[236] Dean, *Opera Seria*, p. 33.
[237] Ibid. p. 142.

We are aware that by August 27th, 1734 from his letter to Sir Knatchbull, Handel intimated he had agreed upon some form of business engagement with Rich:

Sir,

At my arrival in Town from the Country, I found my self honoured of your kind invitation.

I am sorry that by the situation of my affairs I see myself deprived of receiving that pleasure being engaged with Mr. Rich to carry on the Operas at Covent Garden. {…}[238]

Handel commenced work on *Ariodante* on August 12th, 1734, and completed it on October 24th, 1734;[239] Dean thereby concluded Handel had no knowledge of his forthcoming move until the last moment, and discovered the availability of the dance troupe when he finished the autograph of Act II on September 9th.[240]

However, Sarah McCleave, who has extensively researched the autograph scores in conjunction with past sources, argues in opposition to this accepted theory; she proposed that Handel was fully aware of the ballet troupe before he relocated for she theorised he composed this work with the dance-structure in mind before setting the singers' parts thoroughly.[241] McCleave notes the letter to Knatchbull reveals Handel was planning to join Rich shortly before he had completed Act I and therefore had been informed of the availability of the dancers at that point.[242] She has concluded from

---

[238] Deutsch, p. 369.

[239] Ibid. pp. 369–370.

[240] Dean, *Opera Seria*, pp. 33, 142

[241] See Chapter Five 'Ariodante,' p. 205 onward, in Sarah Y. McCleave, *Dance in Handel's Italian Operas: The Collaboration with Marie Sallé*, PH.D. (University of London, King's College, 1993).

[242] Ibid. p. 217.

her studies that dance was intended as an integral part of the opera from its inception as there is an indication the singers parts were set later than the dances.[243] Therefore, it is evident Handel was not ignorant of his pending relocation.

Moreover, the proposed scenario concerning the five-year subsistence contract between Heidegger and Handel, which we examined earlier, challenges and perhaps invalidates the theory that Handel was suddenly expelled without notice. If Heidegger refused to assist Handel in his last year at the Haymarket, Handel may have realised his time there would not extend beyond the original agreement with the Academy directors concerning the use of the equipment for the five years. This would be obvious with the new Opera of the Nobility forming that year; the promoters of this new venture were once the directors of the Academy, and they could reclaim their equipment when the five years had elapsed. Additionally, Heidegger proved eager to fulfil the wishes of the Academy directors previously when the Second Academy was in the formative stage as we have observed, therefore, he could not rely on support from Heidegger. Obviously, Handel realised it was necessary to secure a new venue and therefore, was not unceremoniously discarded by Heidegger without notification.

Fortunately for Handel, there were two possible theatres for him to proceed to at that time: Lincoln's-Inn-Fields and Covent Garden, both managed by John Rich. Rich had employed a modest chorus, implying that Handel could continue to use this element in his operas. In addition, Marie Sallé and a dance troupe were engaged by Rich, providing further possibilities for greater spectacle than before in his operas. McCleave noted that in the early 1730s Handel included dance as entr'acte entertainments in several of his Second Academy operas, also indicating the move to Covent Garden was not necessarily the main factor for encouragement in this area.[244]

---

[243] Ibid. p. 220.
[244] Ibid. p. 215.

However, Sallé, as a renowned dancer, may have proved to be a promising addition to his operas when Handel recognized the necessity to re-attract his audience, while competing with the rival company who succeeded in engaging the famous castrato, Farinelli. In addition, Handel wished to encourage English opera promoters and he may have surmised Sallé would prove to be an advantage in achieving his aim.

Sallé had a particular interest in opera and McCleave believes this is an important clue regarding Handel and Rich's business engagement. Sallé had written to the Duchess of Richmond circa 1732 and mentioned that:

> {...} Le Sr. Rich etant un homme impoli et injuste dont j'ay souffert trop de mavais traittemens pour faire un engagement de trois années suivant mes petits projets. {...}

> {My closest translation; "Mr. Rich is a rude and unjust man so that I have suffered much from a bad salary [in order] to do an engagement for three years following my small projects."} [245]

Surprisingly, she returned to London to dance for Handel's operas despite the fact she disliked Rich. McCleave suggests Rich may have granted her more artistic independence to encourage her to return, as Sallé was particularly interested in dance reform as well as opera; Handel's involvement and his musical contribution at

---

[245] Letter quoted in full in McCleave, *Dance in Handel's Operas*, pp. 73–75. According to the Goodwood MS 22, Rich had hired Sallé for his pantomimes in previous seasons; it appears she did not enjoy working with him as this letter was written after her return to Paris in 1730–31. She returned to London in 1733. See McCleave's thesis for an account of the seasons she worked for Rich.

Covent Garden may have influenced her decision.[246] McCleave notes Handel, Rich, and Sallé recognised the benefits of combining their abilities, and suggests Handel may have planned in advance to join Rich due to the theatrical facilities he could provide.[247]

Exactly how Handel and Rich were introduced remains an enigma. Handel's necessity to secure a new venue possibly indicates he may have initiated the meeting with Rich; however, this cannot be substantiated. Rich was eager to promote new developments regarding English opera, and may have approached Handel. Rich expressed this ideal in a dedication written in 1726 for *The Rape of Proserpine*, which according to McCleave, remained virtually unchanged in the various editions printed then.[248] (See Appendix Seven.)

This dedication is invaluable in illustrating Rich's artistic convictions.[249] First, he described the shortcomings of Italian opera, stating that it was devoid of many scenic elements he wished to see incorporated into that genre. He mentioned the expense associated with the necessity to employ foreign artists, and complained of the subscription system in which "we grow tired of in a few years." It is debatable how Rich viewed Handel's actions concerning the premiere of *Deborah* in this instance; Handel was in effect usurping the subscription system and this may have attracted Rich's attention.

Rich also admitted his desire to see modified works conducted by "an abler Hand." Smith states Handel's admirers believed his music had the,

{...} morally elevating power required of great

---

246   Ibid. p. 75

247   Ibid. p. 75–76.

248   Ibid. pp. 60–62.

249   For an account of John Rich's other interests concerning the theatre culture of London, see the article by Clive Chapman, 'Sir, it will not do!; John Rich and Covent Garden's Early Years,' *Musical Times*, 123 (1982): pp. 831–835.

art, and that through it he could achieve the reform of private and public morals and manners, and unite the nation harmoniously.[250]

While this conviction is more applicable to the development of oratorios, we cannot entirely exclude this concept from the realm of opera. Is it possible Rich deduced that Handel was the composer with the "abler Hand" who would develop a genre England could be proud of? In his conclusion of the dedication Rich states "and do engage, for my own Part, that whenever the Publick Taste shall be disposed to return to the Works of the *Drama*, no one shall rejoice more sincerely than myself." Handel's return to scenic-orientated magic opera with *Orlando*, his first public performances of works with English texts, and his gradual inclusion of chorus, may have indicated the signs Rich anticipated concerning the new disposition of the "Publick's Taste." While it remains inconclusive who initiated the meeting, we may assume Handel and Rich realised a musical collaboration would be mutually beneficial.

John Rich and Handel's Collaboration

In contrast to Handel's partnership with Heidegger where further evidence is available, the arrangements concerning Handel and Rich's collaboration have remained virtually undisclosed, as documents pertaining to their venture are few and far between. Handel, as we have observed, failed to describe the nature of their venture as he simply stated, "being engaged with Mr. Rich to carry on the Operas at Covent Garden." Mainwaring's account relates Handel and Rich entered into a partnership,[251] and Shaftsbury

---

[250] Smith, *Oratorios*, p. 70.
[251] Mainwaring, p. 116.

confirmed this information.[252] Rich stated in a letter to the Duke of Bedford on March 9th, 1737 Handel had caused him "Severe Losses" which prevented him from paying the ground rent on the theatre and on his other properties.[253]

This limited evidence suggests they arranged a provisional agreement similar to the partnership Handel previously entered into with Heidegger. Hume proposed there is evidence the accounts for the opera/oratorio venture with Handel at Covent Garden were recorded as separate accounts from Rich's general bookkeeping.[254] Hume states according to these accounts, there are indications that an arrangement existed between them where they considered certain expenses as fixed charges with preference in payment, and they shared risks and hypothetical profits for the musical sector of the theatre company.[255] While evidence remains inconclusive in this area, their undertaking displays an agreement resembling Handel's arrangement with Heidegger and their "subsistence" plan.

Scholars have questioned why Rich offered Covent Garden to Handel while Lincoln's-Inn-Fields was available, as his pantomime troupe occupied the former. It was a curious arrangement as Rich granted Handel the use of the theatre on designated nights for his operas, and he paid his own actors when they were not working at the theatre.[256] Hume also points out Rich's theatre company did not transfer to Lincoln's-Inn on the nights Handel produced his operas although it remained unoccupied. Hume mentions for the fifty-four nights Handel produced operas at Covent Garden in the 1734–35 season, Lincoln's-Inn offered entertainment for only eleven of those nights.[257] Moreover, all eleven nights were benefit performances,

---

252 Hume, "Handel and Opera Management," p. 354.
253 Ibid.
254 Ibid.
255 Ibid.
256 Ibid. p. 355.
257 Ibid.

implying Rich realised no profit.[258]   Hume suggests that although Rich may have allowed his actors to use the older theatre, he may not have participated with the risk or share in the profits from their productions.[259]   Rich may have anticipated Handel would generate substantial revenue from his operas, which would enable him to pay his actors out of his own pocket, and this may account for his "Severe losses."

It has been questioned why John Rich would be willing to risk his capital on a venture with Handel. In his dedication, Rich mentions that notwithstanding the fact he was realising substantial profits from his pantomimes, he would "rejoice" when public favour returned to serious genres. His eagerness for the production of English opera could have nurtured this optimistic outlook towards his partnership with Handel, considered by many as England's best composer. Apparently disregarding a practical business approach on this one project, he may have decided to afford every opportunity to Handel. Rich aspired to succeed in overcoming the deficiencies in Italian opera he listed in his dedication; allowing Handel the use of the scenery and new machinery at Covent Garden would have been mutually advantageous.

The Opera of the Nobility had previously occupied Lincoln's-Inn-Fields, and it is possible they could have used the sets that were available for their productions, or, they may have cast aside some of their sets when they vacated. Although these are mere conjectures, with either possibility, the implications still exist that if Handel transferred to Lincoln's-Inn, he would have incurred considerable expense in the construction of new scenery, or be forced to use the older sets that his competitors abandoned, and this would have impaired the reception of his productions. The construction of Covent Garden was completed in 1732, incorporating all new sets and scenery with the most up to date machinery, and this may prove

---

[258]   Ibid.
[259]   Ibid.

to be the major factor Rich allowed Handel to remain in the first instance. Essentially, by allowing Handel the use of Covent Garden, Rich may have removed the immediate necessity to provide new sets and costumes for Lincoln's-Inn thus eliminating some of the initial expenses, although new scenery was later constructed for Handel's operas at Covent Garden.

This scenery must have been spectacular indeed with the additional new machinery. Dean and Knapp listed the equipment available at Covent Garden and described a number of the sets from Handel's operas:

> Back-flats, wings, borders, cloudings, transparencies, and columns to Fame's temple for *Giustino*, a ground piece, wings, 'the compass border', and a pyramid for *Atalanta*, and a whole range of special features for *Ariodante*, which though not a magic opera had one of the most splendid productions of the period. They included eight moonlight wings for Act II and a palace with staircases and a gallery for the stage orchestra, with its own wings and borders, in the last scene. The mass of machinery on and under the stage — pulleys, chains, ropes, swivels, cogs, weights, scaffolds — included 'the great counterpoize to all the traps and iron hooks 487lb', 'the counterpoize to front lamps 170lb', and barrels for operating the cylinders that represented the heaving of the sea on the back stage.[260]

Therefore, Handel's necessity to secure a new venue and face the difficulty of maintaining his operas initially proved advantageous. He could continue to use a chorus in his operas, and also had the additional attraction of the famous dancer Sallé with

---

[260] Dean and Knapp, *Handel's Operas*, pp. 24–25. See also Deutsch, p. 579.

excellent sets and a fresh start in a new theatre which his competitors had not previously occupied; importantly, Rich and Sallé appeared enthusiastic about this new venture. Now that Handel was re-established, he resumed his anglicization process with Italian opera, and this proved to be problematic as English preferences had evolved from his early days of *Rinaldo*. Handel would confront great difficulty, which obviously proved to be a grave disappointment.

The Development of Handel's Operas

Ariodante was the first opera Handel composed specifically for Covent Garden, although it would not be premiered until after *Terpsichore / Il Pastor Fido* and *Oreste*. This delay is unusual; if Handel was composing this work for Covent Garden, why did he not produce it directly, particularly as he appeared to have immense pride in it? Handel presented it to the King on the 4th of November 1734, approximately one week after its completion.[261] Handel's strategy in delaying its premiere seems based on tactical consideration in addition to his artistic aims.

Primarily, Handel was compelled to devise a battle plan to compete with the Opera of the Nobility company that had succeeded in engaging the castrato Farinelli, which he had failed to accomplish during the Second Academy. This was a formidable *coup*, and Handel had to skilfully outwit his rivals, while endeavouring to appease a wider audience; as mentioned, he had to regain his previous patrons, including those supporters desiring a form of English opera or other similar genre. Handel's subsequent productions at Covent Garden seems to imply he attempted to combine the two requests in a gradual process to where both

---

[261] Mentioned in an article printed in the *London Daily Post*, Deutsch, p. 372.

audiences would be encouraged to attend, and *Ariodante* apparently was intended to be the main focal point.

Deciding not to open the season of 1734–35 with *Ariodante*, Handel once again revised *Il Pastor Fido* and added the French-style prologue *Terpsichore*. This was Handel's only French opera-ballet production, which seems lamentable today, yet apparently Handel had other plans in progress and did not want to continue with ballet proper; perhaps Handel intended to produce a once-off novelty. Notably his return to pastoral forms apparently originated with the Arcadian influenced Italians re-entering the scene with the production of Bononcini's serenata at the Haymarket in 1732; the revival of *Il Pastor Fido* may have been related to this pastoral "reawakening".

There is also a further possibility which we may add to this observation; Handel may have endeavoured to illustrate he could continue to provide what the directors of the Royal Academy had failed to achieve so many years earlier, i.e. to have operas with all elements, Italian and French, and a troupe for dance as a *permanent feature* of the company, as observed in the Royal Academy Subscriber's Prospectus circa April 1719, and the minutes of December 2nd, 1719:

(From the Subscriber's Prospectus)

> As the Operas themselves will be in greater Perfection that [sic] what have hitherto appeared (Joyning what is excellent both in the French and Italian Theatre) so they will undoubtedly procure better Audiences And by the Constancy and Regularity of the Performance the Taste rendred more universall.[262]

(From the minutes of December 2, 1719)

---

[262] Milhous and Hume, 'New Light On Handel and the Royal Academy,' p. 167.

That Mr Bruce be desir'd to get Mr Labie [L'Abbé] to give A proposal sometime next week in relation to Dancers for the Opera.[263]

We are aware a number of Handel's operas during the Royal Academy featured dance between the acts; dance was also performed integrally within *Numitore* (1720), *Radamisto* (1720), and *Admeto* (1727).[264]   However, this element was expensive and may explain why the directors could not maintain this attraction permanently in the company.   Prefiguring the Royal Academy, a small number of Handel's operas in London had integral dance as opposed to entr'acte entertainments (*Rinaldo* 1711 and 1717, *Teseo* 1713, *Amadigi* 1715); therefore we observe the English previously expressed their desire to have dance included within opera.[265]   Sallé had danced with her brother, perhaps between the acts, during a revival of *Rinaldo* (1717) when she was only nine or ten.[266]   Handel may have planned to encourage all of his previous patrons to return with the availability of Sallé and the dance troupe at Covent Garden; also, the recent addition of chorus within his works was important for this purpose.   Thus, Handel retaliated with *his coup* by producing *Terpsichore* and using their practise of assimilating different cultures in response to their successful engagement of Farinelli.

Already we notice a change regarding Handel's method of structuring his operas; *Terpsichore* features an opening chorus following the overture, and a finale chorus.   In *Il Pastor Fido*, he used dance and chorus to construct a climactic finale.   McCleave mentions Handel's eagerness to add substantial new material for the

---

[263]   Ibid. p. 153.
[264]   McCleave, *Dance in Handel's Operas*, see f., p. 109.
[265]   Ibid.
[266]   Deutsch, p. 75.

dancers highlights his interest in working with them and Sallé.[267] In
Act I of *Il Pastor Fido*, there are several dances and a chorus
included in the hunters' scene, in Act II the chorus precedes the
ballet, and in Act III, the chorus follows the sinfonia and the ballet
at the conclusion; in addition, there is a chorus of High Priests,
which is reminiscent of oratorio.[268] McCleave notes it was common
practise during the early eighteenth century to introduce dance in
opera relating to the different character-types, and the same applies
to the use of dance in *Il Pastor Fido*. For instance, the chorus and
dances of the huntsmen reflect Silvio's love of hunting in contrast to
romantic love;[269] thereby, Handel used dance to reflect and enhance
the drama.

In addition, Handel apparently experimented with duets by
extending their diversity; in *Terpsichore*, there are three duets
featuring Apollo and Erato as they comment upon and compliment
the muse's skill as she dances. This proportion of duets within a
relatively short work indicates a departure from the traditional solo
of the *da capo* aria. In *Il Pastor Fido* there are two duets with
Mirtillo and Amarilli as they meet their fate heightening the tension
of the drama and later the release of that tension as the story is

---

[267] McCleave, *Dance in Handel's Operas*, p. 133.

[268] Dean observes this finale displays Handel's technique of modifying
the formal structure of *opera seria* for dramatic purposes. Dean states;
"The climax of *Il Pastor Fido*, an opera scarcely remarkable for the tautness
of the plot, is a duet of farewell for two lovers, one of whom has been
condemned to death on a false charge of adultery. The duet leads without
a break into an orchestral symphony as the priests make a solemn entry to
claim their victim, and this in turn, by means of an abrupt progression, to
an arioso for the High Priest, ordering the sacrifice to stop. Then at last
there is some recitative explaining why he takes this course, after which he
repeats his arioso, extending the scene and producing another variant of da
capo form. The repeat was a refinement of Handel's; it is not in the
libretto." Dean, p. 171.

[269] Ibid. p. 148.

resolved with a happy conclusion. This heightening and releasing of dramatic tension with his signal use of duets would become a feature of his Covent Garden operas.

Handel's attempt to fulfil English expectations regarding spectacle with his significant inclusion of ballet must have proved irritating to the Italians. Strohm mentions that libretto reformers, especially the Arcadian Zeno, rejected ballets in *opera seria* as impure elements.[270] Rolli apparently agreed with his idol's views, for he wrote this letter on the same day of the premiere of *Terpsichore – Il Pastor Fido:*

Rolli to Riva in Vienna

London, 9th November 1734.

I know that you would have liked me to give you the latest theatre news, but although I did take some part therein last year, and may do so this year, I am so disgusted by it all that I do not care to talk about it, let alone write about it, {...}[271]

On the same day, the *Ipswich Gazette* printed a notice referring to Handel's "fine English voice," i.e. the singer Mr. Beard.[272] Handel was enthusiastic concerning this English singer according to Lady Elizabeth Compton's letter to Countess Elizabeth Shirley on November 21st, 1734:

A Scholar of Mr Gates, Beard, {...} shines in the Opera of Covent Garden & Mr Hendell is so full of his Praises that he says he will surprise the Town with his

---

[270] Strohm, *Dramma per Musica*, p. 263.
[271] Deutsch, p. 374.
[272] Ibid.

performances before the Winter is over.[273]

Handel would continue to employ English performers in the future; in addition to placating the English demand for native genres and performers, English singers were less expensive than their Italian counterparts and their employment may have been a necessity as well as an advantage.

It is difficult to determine what measure of success Handel achieved with this first endeavour. Deutsch's documentary biography does not contain a printed record indicating the public's reaction or approval; in addition, Sallé's efforts with Handel are not documented, which is particularly frustrating. There is, however, an indication printed in Deutsch that Sallé was accepted equally with Farinelli according to this article in *Le Pour et Contre*, Paris [June?] 1735:

> Mademoiselle Sallé, who had at first been favourably received by the English as Farinelli {...}[274]

There is little mention of Handel's first production for Covent Garden or Sallé's performance following this article. McCleave noticed however, Handel and Sallé's collaboration in 1734–35 created an impression with the public, for several of the dances from *Il Pastor Fido* and *Terpsichore* were published with other dances from the same season in the sixth book of *The Lady's Banquet*, and this edition is the first example of Walsh publishing dance music from London opera.[275] One of the dances from *Il Pastor Fido* became a popular entr'acte dance as Glover's *The Faithful Shepherd*, February 22nd, 1735, which was repeated on ten occasions during that year, and was also performed in 1740.[276]

---

[273] Ibid. p. 375.
[274] Ibid. p. 390.
[275] McCleave, *Dance in Handel's Operas*, p. 154.
[276] Ibid. p. 155.

Therefore, there are indications the public received Handel's efforts with a measure of enthusiasm.

Handel's subsequent productions featured the revival of *Arianna in Creta*, and his new pasticcio *Oreste*. He revived *Arianna* in November of 1734, and presented it with several new arias and dances, yet it did not equal the success of the previous season. McCleave mentions Handel may not have discovered the formula with which to compete with Farinelli at this point, and would later be more successful with *Ariodante* and *Alcina*.[277] The autograph scores of *Arianna* are confusing according to McCleave as the conducting and harpsichord scores do not present a complete record of the dances that were included; for example, the dances for Act II are not extant in these scores, yet the libretto indicates dance.[278] In addition, the conducting score does not contain the Act III dances and the harpsichord score features only the bass line.[279] However, these dances were included in *Oreste* and *Alcina*; two of the Act III dances, i.e. the gavotte and the 6/8 dance, were used in *Oreste*, the third, a musette, was included in the overture for *Alcina* and Act III of *Oreste*.[280] McCleave relates in her thesis Handel may have simply detached dances from one opera and transferred them to the next one he was working on.[281] This not only suggests haste on Handel's part, but also the general success of his dance music: this use of borrowed material in repeated succession with regard to production indicates the dance music must have proved popular if he was prepared to reuse it within a brief period of time.

Handel's decision to revive this work may relate to his inclusion of scenic dream scenes in his first production,[282] and he may have wished to capitalise on this element again. This first

---

277 Ibid. p. 160.
278 Ibid. p. 170–171.
279 Ibid. p. 171.
280 Ibid.
281 Ibid. op. cit.
282 Ibid. p. 167.

supernatural scene features Theseus who falls asleep outside a temple. The personification of Sleep appears to Theseus on a cloud as an old man who conjures dreams that materialise as winged human-like figures; when Sleep disappears, Theseus dreams of fighting the Minotaur.[283]   However, it is uncertain if Handel included dance in his first version of *Arianna*, but it has been suggested he added these scenes for the revival due to the English partiality for supernatural and magical settings.

His next opera *Oreste* is distinctive as it is a pasticcio based on his own music rather than material or operas composed by others.[284] This self-borrowing is not an unusual trait for Handel as it is accepted he borrowed frequently from his previous works, however, the fact *Oreste* contains all of his own music suggests Handel was proceeding with caution. His earlier pasticcios based on music by Vinci and Hasse during the Second Academy, as we have noted, were unfavourably received, and Handel obviously learned from his past miscalculations. He also included sections of newly composed music, i.e. the recitatives, the two accompangnati, and possibly the two ballet dances nos. 11 and 13, as there are no models yet discovered for these two dances.[285] This time his pasticcio was more successful:

From the "Bee", 21st December 1724

Last night their Majesties were at the Theatre
Royal in Covent Garden, to see the Opera of Orestes,

---

[283] Ibid.

[284] George Friederich Handel, *Oreste; opera in tre atti*, HWV A[11] (Hallische Händel-Ausgabe edition, Kritische Gesamtausgabe, Bärenreiter Kassel, BA 4045, 1991): p.XVI.

[285] Ibid. p. XXII. According to the editor, Baselt, the claim made by Chrysander that three of the arias (presumably nos. 1, 3, and 21), and the overture were all newly composed is misleading as they are arrangements of earlier pieces.

which was perfom'd with great Applause.[286]

Bernd Baselt, editor of the Hallische Händel-Ausgabe edition of *Oreste*, suggested all of the dances in the opera were included later "since its conducting score distinctly shows that the ballet numbers at the end of all three acts were later additions."[287] However, McCleave observed if the dances were later additions, Handel allowed space in the manuscript for their inclusion, suggesting he had planned to add dance at an earlier date even if he had not yet decided upon the final structure and details.[288] The libretto and the musical sources according to McCleave do not give detailed instructions concerning the dances; primary music material is supplied, but without further information.[289] According to newspaper reports, one dance sequence was entitled the *Grecian Sailor*;[290] the report alleges men performed the dance, although McCleave stated it is difficult to determine the actual identity of the Act II dancers.[291] It is possible Sallé participated in this dance, for the Air and dance in 3/8 time from *Terpsichore* in which Sallé performed were borrowed for the sailor dances.[292] Baselt brings to our attention the important repetition in the opera of Iphigenia's warning to the Greeks that their path of escape from Thoas' guards was to set sail for the open sea;[293] he proposed for productions today, a suitable backdrop for this action would consist of a screen or projection depicting the sea, or ships at anchor in order to

---

[286] Deutsch, p. 377.

[287] *Oreste; opera in tre atti*, HWV A[11], p. XVIII

[288] McCleave, *Dance in Handel's Operas*, p. 187.

[289] Ibid. p. 191.

[290] See the entry for April 17th, April 1735 in Deutsch, p. 387.

[291] McCleave, *Dance in Handel's Operas*, p. 192.

[292] Ibid.

[293] *Oreste; opera in tre atti*, HWV A[11], p. XXIII.

maintain the symbolism of the drama.[294] The Sailor's Dance may have had a similar function in Handel's time; hence, it is possible the dance portrayed important imagery in relation to the drama which the audience would have appreciated.

Handel's diminution concerning the use of chorus in *Oreste* when compared with his earlier works is obvious; there is a brief chorus in the penultimate scene where the populace shout "Kill the tyrant," followed by a sinfonia reflecting the battle taking place off stage.[295] (See Example 3.) The opera also concludes with a choral-finale, however, Handel did not include chorus in Act I nor Act II; was he testing the audience to determine the extent of their appreciation of chorus? Handel's slight retreat from using this element suggests he was returning to his former style of the Royal Academy days. Lowell Lindgren mentions the only spectacle Handel's Royal Academy operas contained were "the perfunctory battles and processions that were typical of heroic works,"[296] and Handel's application of chorus in *Oreste* is similar to this convention.

---

[294] Ibid.

[295] Ibid. p. 126.

[296] Lowell Lingren, 'The Staging of Handel's Operas in London,' in *Handel; Tercentenary Collection*, ed. Stanley Sadie and Anthony Hicks, (Hong Kong: Macmillan Press Ltd., 1987), p. 98.

Example 3   Act III, Scene VII from *Oreste.*

Which faction was Handel attempting to appeal to, his Italian or English opera-preferring public? Obviously, he endeavoured to attract both sectors; the Greek-Arcadian setting would have been popular with both audiences, for the English had adopted Athenian tragedy, and the Italians would have approved of the Arcadian myth. In addition, Handel had retained the use of dance integral to the plot of the drama, which might appeal to English audiences as the obvious nautical aspect of the Sailor's Dance evokes a typical British theme. However, using the chorus for minimal effect in *Oreste*

could have been his method to attract the chorus-wary Italians and introduce them gradually to its beneficial use in opera. Therefore, Handel was experimenting with various conventions in an effort to unite the two factions.

Handel's project experienced a sudden transition at this point; McCleave notes that with the exception of *Jupiter in Argos*, (which had only two performances in May 1739), *Oreste* had the shortest run of any of Handel's pasticcios — only three performances. Short runs were considered normal with Handel's pasticcios, yet this unusually brief production period seems rather peculiar and does not configure with the "great Applause" the documents of the day recorded.[297] Perhaps the revival of *Ottone* on December 10th, 1734, produced by the Opera of the Nobility was responsible for this disappointing outcome.[298] Burney stated that the Nobility company revived *Handel's* opera *Ottone*,[299] and this unauthorised pirate production may have forced Handel to alter his agenda. What an unusual predicament — it was a masterstroke if not a warning, not to mention an astute strategic move. In effect, the Opera of the Nobility members were informing Handel not only were all the Italians united, they no longer required his services as they could produce his music, and thereby simultaneously ridiculed his practise of producing pasticcios. This action apparently resulted in public embarrassment for Handel.

Possibly, *Oreste* was nearing completion and under rehearsal at this point, and Handel may have been compelled to proceed with its production only eight days later on the 18th of December as he could not immediately launch a proper counterattack. One member of the public not sympathetic towards Handel highlighted his embarrassing situation:

---

[297] McCleave, *Dance in Handel's Operas*, pp. 180–181.
[298] Deutsch, p. 376.
[299] Ibid. pp. 376–377.

From a Letter, Probably Written to Catherine Collingwood

Bullstrode [Street], Dec. 27, 1734.

I don't pity Handell in the least, for I hope this mortification will make him a human creature; for I am sure before he was no better than a brute, when he could treat civilized people with so much brutality as I know he has done.[300]

As the Opera of the Nobility would not produce their next work *Polifemo* until February 1st, 1735,[301] and because *Oreste* had been performed on December 18th, 1734, the letter obviously refers to these unexpected circumstances concerning the revival of *Ottone* in opposition to Handel. Evidently, the public remained incensed with the initial "*Deborah* incident" and Handel's unceremonious dismissal of Senesino.

Handel would now be compelled to address this challenge inflicted upon him and his work; perhaps this is exactly what his competitors were hoping to achieve. The revival of *Ottone* by the Opera of the Nobility may have been designed to ascertain what Handel had previously composed, but for an undisclosed reason, decided to delay its premiere.

The composition of *Ariodante* had been accomplished for some time; as mentioned previously, Handel presented *Ariodante* to the King on November 4th, 1734 according to an article in the *London Daily Post*. This assuredly created curiosity with his competitors as this work was assuming the aspect of a highly

---

[300] Ibid. p. 378.
[301] Ibid. p. 437

classified project. According to the tone of the article, Handel's audience with the King relating to *Ariodante* was not for a rehearsal, suggesting an immediate production was not forthcoming; [302] "When Mr. Handel waited on their Majesties with his new Opera [...]."[303] What was the exceptional quality or factor concerning *Ariodante* that would prompt Handel to present it to the King, and then paradoxically withhold its production? Was he postponing *Ariodante*'s premiere for a specific occasion? Perhaps the curiosity-seeking rivals attempted to provoke Handel into producing his "classified project" with their pirate production of *Ottone*.

Supporting this theory is the fact *Oreste* did not survive past three performances despite its moderate success before *Ariodante*'s premiere; it would seem illogical to halt a production that was receiving "Great Applause," therefore the pirate production of *Ottone* obviously distracted Handel. What is intriguing, when Handel produced *Ariodante* on January 8th, 1735, his rivals never again produced his works in competition with him. Either they were obliged to submit to his musical dominance, or, their possible aim with respect to *Ottone*, i.e. to incite Handel into producing his reserved work, *Ariodante*, had been accomplished. As a result, Handel had apparently produced his *pièce de résistance* before he had prepared the London public for its introduction.

Ariodante is an amazing contrast to *Oreste* with regard to its structural features. This abrupt change in progression suggests Handel may have intended to gradually introduce an amalgamated style of Italian-English opera, but was compelled to advance his agenda due to his competitors' production of his *Ottone*. Strohm noted the obvious contrast between *Oreste* and *Ariodante:*

> And in the area of libretto and dramatic subject, the character of *Ariodante* as a chivalric and pastoral

---

[302]   It was common practise for the supporters of an opera to attend rehearsals.

[303]   Deutsch, p. 372.

play with 'romantic ingredients' — a description requiring verification — would seem to contrast sharply with the classicist-rationalist character of *Oreste*, emphasized by Bernd Baselt.[304]

Dean mentioned, "unlike other operas based on Renaissance epics it has no supernatural or magic content."[305] Dean was also unable to classify *Ariodante* into his heroic or anti-heroic categories and stated the libretto is almost unique for its time in that it did not feature a subplot.[306]

Astonishingly, this drama is set in Scotland, a country far removed from the setting of ancient Greece in *Oreste*, however, the pastoral ideal is not lost as Strohm relates Scotland was stereotyped as an "underdeveloped pastoral community," and "the same country generates beautiful gardens, vales, shepherdesses and betrothal dances, {…}."[307]

For instance, at the conclusion of Act I, nymphs and shepherds are invited by Ariodante to dance and join in the happy celebration held in honour of his betrothal to Ginevra, and thus create momentum for the finale of Act I. In addition, the fantastic, albeit not magical, element of pastoral forms is represented by Ginevra's dream scene danced as a ballet sequence at the end of Act II. Thus, Handel may have been attempting to introduce opera with an English setting without dismissing the current popularity of pastorals. Dean also remarked:

> It {the score} also reflects Handel's intense love
> for the countryside, which goes far beyond the demands
> of the pastoral convention and emerges most clearly in
> his setting of Milton's *L'Allegro* and *Il Penseroso* and in

---

[304] Strohm, *Dramma per Musica*, p. 257.
[305] Dean, *Opera Seria*, p. 102.
[306] Ibid.
[307] Strohm, *Dramma per Musica*, p. 267.

late oratorios like *Solomon* and *Susanna*. Many of his operas contain garden or woodland scenes, often at night, and they are quite different in atmosphere from his interiors. In *Ariodante* more than half of the action takes place in the open air. The second act begins with a little ten-bar sinfonia depicting night and the rising of the moon over the palace garden. {See Example 4.} It is an incomparable piece of tone-painting and a vivid stoke of dramatic irony: with Polinesso on the stage, it prepares the background for the cruel deception of Ariodante by the false Ginevra. The moonrise was introduced by Handel; it is not in the source libretto.[308]

Example 4.

Act II, Scene I — Sinfonia from *Ariodante*.

[308] Dean, *Opera Seria*, p. 103.

We have already noted how the Arcadian-Italians had centred their ideals upon pastoral conventions and Handel's endeavour to attract and encourage this section of his audience to return. Moreover, we are reminded of the statements printed in *The Touchstone* of 1728 suggesting the methods that would reconcile English audiences to the Italian language, which we may deem apropos concerning the setting of *Ariodante*. Irving Lowens quotes this suggestion from the *Touchstone* as follows:

> The second go-around begins with a suggestion to the directors of the Royal Academy that "if they would but allow some extraordinary Events either historical or traditionary (which wholly regard our selves) to be translated into *Italian*, [21]'" the English, being great patriots, would forget about their objections to the Italian language. "I'll engage for my Countrymen they'll resign the Language for the History," the author writes, "that being undoubtedly originally our own, and the English Page always leading in the Opera Books, we gain the disputed Punctilio, and bring off our Honour safe, which is dearer to every *True Briton* than Life, [21–22.]"[309]

Notwithstanding that *Ariodante* had been adapted from an earlier libretto by Antonio Salvi and was not based on an English text, the fact Handel would select a plot set within the British Isles is quite fascinating. In addition, Handel seems to have taken considerable care with its composition; Strohm related that, "Signs of an aesthetic reorientation might be discovered in the rarely noted fact that *Ariodante* does not contain a single musical borrowing from earlier works by Handel."[310]

---

* P. 21 of *The Touchstone*.

309 Lowens, 'The Touch-Stone,' *Musical Quarterly*, p. 333.

310 Strohm, *Dramma per Musica*, p. 257

There are further indications Handel was extending the *opera seria* convention beyond his previous experiments, for example, his innovations with regard to the duets. In Act I, Ariodante and Ginevra are assigned two duets: "Prendi da questa mano il pegno," and "Se rinasce nel mio caro." The first duet concentrates on the couple's engagement, and at the conclusion of Act I the second duet displays their happiness as they celebrate this joyful occasion. Handel includes an unusual innovation to the first duet when the King, Ginevra's father, literally interrupts them in recitative and wishes to take both their hands as they pledge their troth and share in their joy. (Scene VI.) This again displays Handel's ability to extend the boundaries of recitative in a manner befitting the action of the drama. (See Example 5.) Dean has analysed this duet as follows:

> Ariodante, alone in the garden, sings of his love in an arioso of haunting beauty, richly accompanied by oboes and five-part strings (three violins). Ginevra appears, and he tells her in recitative that he is too humble to ask for her hand. In a touching phrase, without preliminary ritornello, she offers it to him ("Prendi da questa mano"). This is the start of the duet, but the fact is concealed till eight bars later, when Ariodante enters in the dominant and takes her hand ("Prendo"). After a regular second part Handel inserts a little two-bar ritornello to introduce the da capo. But now there are two surprises. Ariodante, confident of Ginevra's love, answers her after one bar instead of eight; and two bars later the duet is broken off by the King, her father, who comes in behind, takes both their hands, and gives them his blessing in recitative, the action continuing without a break. {Example 5.}
>
> The whole scene is a miracle of art, achieved by the simplest means. This is the first time we meet any of the characters except Ginevra; yet by the end we

167

know all about their relationship. There are no da capos and therefore no exits. Everything builds up to the King's interruption, which coming just as we reach the expected da capo achieves the maximum surprise; {...}.[311]

Example 5.

"Prendi da questo mano" from *Ariodante.* Bars 80–84.

We find the next two duets in Act III; the first duet "Spera, spera io gia mi pento / Dite spera, e son contento" assigned to Dalinda, Givenra's lady in waiting, and Lurcanio, Ariodante's brother, is of particular interest. Lurcanio is hopeful that in time Dalinda will learn to love him and not Polinesso; Dean stated that Dalinda and Lurcanio's duet is unique for it is the only duet composed for a tenor voice in all of Handel's London operas.[312] Of particular interest, the nature of the duet is concealed from our aural perception as it commences as a tenor aria and Dalinda does not enter until thirty-seven bars later.[313] Dean states this design matched the action:

---

[311] Dean, *Opera seria*, pp. 104–105.
[312] Ibid. p. 106.
[313] Ibid.

Hitherto, Dalinda, infatuated with Polinesso, has refused to look at Lurcanio. Her eyes have been opened to the fact that Polinesso has been using her for his own purposes, but she is inhibited by shame. In this long duet Lurcanio gently woos and wins her.[314]

Hence, Dalinda's delayed entry in the duet magnifies the exchange of emotion between the two characters. The last duet is reserved for Ariodante and Ginevra as they rejoice in their happy reunion.

In comparison with *Oreste*, the sudden reintroduction of climactic finales at the end of each act is surprising; for example, in Act I, Ariodante and Ginevra's second duet is integrated with the chorus and ballet of nymphs and shepherds. They sing in F major in the tempo of a gavotte, and the following ballet repeats the gavotte. McCleave mentions this gavotte has a dual function as it proclaims their love and the uncertain future with all of its hidden trials.[315] McCleave remarks audiences of the day would have recognised that the early celebration within the drama signalled pending difficulties for the happy couple, and is similar to the function of the gavotte in the Act II finale of *Il Pastor Fido*.[316] Dean also mentions:

> The first finale in *Ariodante*, with its ballet and chorus, may be one of the rare exceptions to the rule that the curtain did not drop between the acts, though the license seems to have been used to reveal a spectacular or crowded scene rather than to close one.[317]

The finale of Act III is similar to Act I, as Ariodante and

---

[314] Ibid.
[315] McCleave, *Dance in Handel's Operas*, p. 234.
[316] Ibid. pp. 234–235.
[317] Dean, *Opera Seria*, pp. 142–143.

Ginevra's duet is included with the chorus and ballet of knights, ladies, and general populace to conclude the scene with a climax. In addition, the last dance movement is musically identical to the second chorus.

Finale Sequences of Acts I and II

Act I Finale Sequence
Sinfonia
<u>Ginevra & Ariodante - *Duetto*</u>: "Se rinasce nel mio cor"
<u>Coro</u>   "Se godete al vostro amor"
Il Ballo

Act III Finale Sequence
Sinfonia
<u>Ginevra & Ariodante – *Duetto*</u>: "Bramo haver mille
                                        vite/cori, per consacrarli
                                        a te"
<u>Coro</u>   "Ogn' uno acclami bella
                                         virtute"
Il Ballo
<u>Coro</u>   "Sa trionfar ogn' or
                                         virtute ogni cor"

As previously observed, the sets for *Ariodante* were extremely elaborate and obviously enhanced the production enormously; an on-stage orchestra accompanied the Act III chorus and dance segment taking place on a balcony.[318] McCleave also concluded

---

[318] Handel included an onstage (or behind-stage) orchestra for only three operas; *Ariodante*, *Deidamia* and *Giulio Cesare*. See Dean, *Opera Seria*, p. 196.

from her studies of the precursors to Handel's version of *Ariodante* the final scenes to Acts I and III were new additions for this London production.[319]

However, there is a question concerning the dances of Act II as the ballet of Act II was removed from the original autograph of *Ariodante* and partly copied in *Alcina*.[320] These dances for Act II, representing Ginevra's troubled dreams, were intended to be performed when she learns of Ariodante's supposed death; she is repudiated by her father and she fails to understand the basis for his anger. However, Ginevra is innocent as Polinesso, who is in love with her, devised a plan to discredit her love for Ariodante whereby he would abandon her. Polinesso tricked Dalinda into dressing as Ginevra and rendezvous with him at night in the garden where they will be discovered by Ariodante, and by so doing he has destroyed Ginevra's reputation. Ginevra has "Benign" and "Malevolent" dreams that engage in an allegorical battle through the medium of dance and thereby illustrate her tumultuous emotional state; these dances are entitled *Entrée des Songes agréables*, *Entrée des Songes funestes*, *Entrés des Songes agréables effrayès*, and *Le combat des Songes funestes et agréables*.

In addition, these dance sequences were not mentioned in the libretto of 1735. Strohm questioned if these dance segments reprinted in the scores today were actually performed at the premiere, as the *Entrée de' Mori-Rondeau* could have been performed in their place.[321] Strohm also states if Handel did decide to use the *Entrée de' Mori* replacing these dream sequences, he may have retreated from an innovation.[322] However, according to McCleave, the *Entrée de' Mori* was included in the conducting and harpsichord scores later and may have been performed for the 1736

---

[319] See McCleave, *Dance in Handel's Operas*, pp. 209–214 for a commentary on the past sources and precursors to Handel's version.

[320] Strohm, *Dramma per Musica*, p. 260.

[321] Ibid.

[322] Ibid.

revival;[323] she also adds the omission of the Act II dances from the 1735 libretto could have been an oversight.[324] This observation seems rational; it would be illogical for Handel to have eliminated a dramatic application of dance for the premiere, particularly when this finale was unique concerning his operas. Dean observed that the second-act finale of *Ariodante* was extremely original:

> In her tragic E minor aria Ginevra {…} begins to doubt her sanity and evokes death to end her sufferings. {She} falls into an exhausted sleep {…}. {Ginevra} wakes in terror, {after the ballet sequence}, and the act ends abruptly with a six-bar accompanied recitative in F sharp minor — the only thing of the kind in any of Handel's operas, though he had experimented with recitative endings, in and out the main key, in several early cantatas. {…}{See Example 6.}
>
> The end with ballet and accompanied recitative seems to have been Handel's idea. It does not occur in the 1718 Venice edition of Salvi's libretto, on which Handel's was based, though the possibility that there was some intermediate version cannot be ruled out.[325]

[323] McCleave, *Dance in Handel's Operas*, pp. 221, 223.
[324] Ibid. p. 228.
[325] Dean, *Opera Seria*, p. 143.

Example 6. Act II Finale recitative.

It is possible Handel substituted the *Entrée de' Mori* if the first version of the second-act finale was not favourably received. However, McCleave has theorised if he had initially decided upon the grotesque dance *Entrée de' Mori* and the rondeau, the theme of the opera would have remained intact although the dances would not have been as integral to the drama as the dream-sequences. Dancing Moors would not only have catered to the interest in exotic dances, but would also have alluded to jealousy and its related vices as *Othello* was performed many times during the 1733–34 and 1734–35 seasons. [326] Both *Ariodante* and *Othello* have similar themes concerning jealousy, therefore the dancing Moors would have been topical in accordance with the current *zeitgeist*.[327] McCleave summarises the importance of dance within *Ariodante*:

> Handel's use of dance in *Ariodante* represented an important departure from typical opera seria practise, and from his operas which were produced

---

[326] McCleave, *Dance in Handel's Operas*, p. 240–241.
[327] Ibid.

earlier in the season. *Ariodante* is the only Handel opera in which new scenes were introduced in order to include extensive sequences of dancing. Although *Arianna*, *Il pastor fido*, and *Oreste* contained considerable amount of dancing, none attempts to integrate the dances into a plot; although *Terpsichore*, arguably, demonstrates a high degree of integration between dance and music, Handel achieved this by adopting a French form, whereas *Ariodante* is essentially a *dramma per musica*.[*][328]

However, Strohm questioned if we may regard *Ariodante* uniquely innovative within the mainstream of Italian *dramma per musica*. Generally, ballets were included with all operatic genres, depending on preferences and resources, and subsequently in the eighteenth century *opera seria* was combined with ballet-pantomimes, which could have an independent subject.[329] Strohm points out that Metastasio's operas *L'Olimpiade* (1733) and *Achille in Sciro* (1736) featured mythological and pastoral scenes with chorus, and Antonio Vivaldi's *Dorilla in Tempe* had three pastoral scenes with dance and chorus.[330] Strohm stated that Handel's *Ariodante* is consistent with the traditions of Italian *dramma per musica*, particularly when we take into account the development of this genre in Germany.[331]

---

[*] McCleave's footnote: "Reinhard Strohm makes a convincing argument for considering *Ariodante* as a dramma per musica in his 'Ariodante; a dramma per musica,' [programme note] G.F. Handel's *Ariodante*, dir. David Alden, cond. Nicholas McGegan, English National Opera, London, April–June 1993 (unpaginated).

[328] Ibid. p. 245.

[329] Strohm, *Dramma per musica*, p. 11.

[330] Ibid. p. 261.

[331] Ibid. See also Ellen T. Harris, *Handel and the Pastoral Tradition*, for an in-depth study regarding Handel's pastoral style and German

Notwithstanding this debate, *Ariodante* stands out distinctively from Handel's London operas, as the quotation from McCleave emphasises above, due to the scale of integrated dance and drama in comparison with his previous operas, particularly those from the Royal Academy days. As mentioned, Handel's operas from the Royal Academy period are generally categorised in the heroic vein. Strohm stated opera was deficient in pastoral settings due to the heroic-historical subject matter of *opera seria* as developed in the latter half of the seventeenth century.[332] Subsequently he points out Kathleen Kuzmick Hansell's observation that the development of the reformed *opera seria* during the two decades from circa 1700 to 1720 featured less ballet integral to the dramatic content, although there were several exceptions.[333] Considering Zeno's rejection of these elements, and Rolli's emulation of Zeno's ideology in conjuction with other reformers, the Royal Academy heroic operas may be perceived as a reflection of this influence. Although Handel did compose dance music for a small number of his Royal Academy works, one can emphatically state that these works could not compare with his developments during his first Covent Garden era. Perhaps the artistic liberty Handel enjoyed at Covent Garden played a particular role; he was no longer obliged to comply with the demands of the Academy directors — Handel was free to indulge in expressing his personal artistic creativity, although it still remained necessary to please the audiences.

Unfortunately, Handel's efforts with *Ariodante* did not meet with success. Queen Caroline wrote the following account in a letter to her daughter Princess Ann on 14th January 1735:

> Handel has not met with his usual approval. They say his opera is so pathetic and lugubrious that everyone who has returned from it has this opinion and

---

traditions.

[332] Ibid. p. 262.
[333] Ibid. p. 263.

has been saddened by it.[334]

Princess Caroline wrote a similar opinion to Princess Anne on the same date:

> Handel presented his opera on Wednesday, fairly full. It is not much approved, being among [his] most pathetic, in the style favoured by his new friend, who, as you know, has the misfortune that his advice is scarcely worth following, in affairs of money as well....[335]

It is regrettable that the public was disappointed with the performance and disapproved of this opera, however, it supports the two observations made earlier. Apparently, the public was not prepared for the introduction of this "pathetic" style, thereby supporting the first observation that Handel had planned to gradually introduce an amalgamated form of *opera seria* and was compelled to change his plans abruptly due to the pirate production of *Ottone* by the rival opera company. The second observation refers to the debates regarding the Act II dances and whether they were performed or not; seemingly Handel may have included the pantomime dances in the premiere performance and may have replaced them with the *Entrée de' Mori* in later performances as a consequence of the adverse reaction from the audience. Notice how Princess Caroline reported Handel had followed the advice of "his friend" — could this have implied John Rich? Rich was renowned for his pantomime productions, and this may indicate "the style" that Princess Caroline was referring to. Accordingly, it would be logical for Handel to have replaced these dances in the suggested

---

[334] McCleave, *Dance in Handel's Operas*, p. 206. As translated by Richard G. King, 'Handel's Travels in the Netherlands in 1750,' *Music and Letters* 72 (1991): p. 384.

[335] Ibid. As translated in King, p. 384.

manner above.

In addition to the obvious lack of public enthusiasm for this opera, Handel had a myriad of other problems to confront. Rumours regarding the opposition of the Prince of Wales to Handel's company as a form of rebellion to his father, a staunch supporter of Handel, seems to have taken its toll, notwithstanding that members of the public remained unforgiving concerning Handel's actions with the production of *Deborah*. We are now aware that this supposed opposition on behalf of the Prince seems exaggerated for existing records indicate that he actually supported Handel.[336] Yet, members of the public continued to foment these rumours of contention, perchance for expedience sake to gather support for the new company in opposition to Handel, and these accusations must have adversely affected both opera companies to some degree. The Prince attended the Opera of the Nobility, thus affording it a fashionable status, however, the King supported Handel, and attending the rival company was to risk incurring Royal disfavour. Lord Hervey mentioned in his memoirs that support of the two companies reflected one's political stance:

> An anti-Handelist was looked upon as an anti-courtier, and voting against the Court in Parliament was hardly a less remissable or more venial sin than speaking against Handel or going to Lincoln's Inn Field's Opera. [337]

However, when Farinelli arrived in London, he drew the crowds to the Nobility Opera, and the fear of displeasing the King was no longer a shield for Handel. In addition, Handel had

---

[336] See McGeary's article 'Handel, Prince Frederick, and the Opera of the Nobility Reconsidered' and Carole Taylor's article 'Handel and Frederick, Prince of Wales,' *Musical Times*, 125 (1984) for a more in-depth account concerning this exaggerated view.

[337] Deutsch, p. 380.

infuriated members of the public with his premiere of *Deborah* and the dismissal of Senesino to such an extent that they retaliated by attending the rival company. Following this disappointing reception of *Ariodante*, Handel revived his oratorio of *Esther* on March 5th, 1735, and introduced his first organ concertos in an attempt to appeal to the English audience; however, despite his praiseworthy music, the public continually refused to attend his productions:

From the "Old Whig;" OR, "The Consistent Protestant".

20th March 1735
A letter to a Friend in the Country

{...} *Farinello* surpasses every thing we have hitherto heard ... 'tis no Wonder that the other Theatres decline. *Handel*, whose excellent Compositions have often pleased our ears and touched out Hearts, has this Winter sometimes performed to an almost empty Pitt. He has lately reviv'd his fine *Oratorio* of *Esther*, in which he has introduced two Concerto's on the Organ that are inimitable. But so strong is the Disgust taken against him, that even this has been far from bringing him crowded Audiences; tho' there were no other publick Entertainments on those Evenings. {...}[338]

Hence, we may conclude Handel created many of his own difficulties as his decisions with *Deborah* fostered sentiments of antipathy with the public. On April 1st, 1735, Handel struggled on in spite of these obstacles and produced the oratorio *Athalia* with a new organ concerto. At this point, the journals of the day are somewhat deceptive in reporting the actual circumstances

---

[338] Ibid. p. 384.

concerning the production and Handel's situation. *The London Daily Post* on April the 3rd, reported the "Youth," i.e. William Savage, was "met with universal Applause."[339] From this report, one might conclude the oratorio was well attended, however, we learn from a later publication that Covent Garden remained virtually empty:

"Le Pour et Contre", Paris [May?] 1735

{...} Mr. Handel has not omitted to produce a new Oratorio, which is given on Wednesdays and Fridays, {...}. He is admired, but from a distance, for he is often alone; a spell draws the crowd to Farinelli's. {...}[340]

Confusion exists with regard to the production of *Alcina*, April 16th. This was one of Handel's successful operas at Covent Garden, and great admiration was expressed for its style and his music. According to Mrs. Pendarves' letter to her mother dated April the 8th, the opera portrayed "a thousand beauties."[341] The *London Daily Post* on the 16th of April reported "Their Majesties intend being at the Opera," and on May 15th reported that the opera was received with great applause.[342] This obviously suggests *Alcina* was more successful with the public in contrast to *Ariodante*, particularly when we consider it had eighteen performances.[343] Evidently, Handel had learned a hard lesson from the public's reaction to *Ariodante* and continued to experiment; he returned to a typical Arcadian setting of ancient Greece with a magical subject for

---

[339] Ibid. p. 385.
[340] Ibid. p. 390.
[341] Ibid. p. 385.
[342] Ibid. pp. 386, 389.
[343] McCleave, *Dance In Handel's Operas*, p. 247.

179

Alcina, and this may account for its relative success.

Yet, other sections of the opera did not meet with audience approval, for instance, Sallé and her ballet where she reportedly danced as Cupid.[344] The audience had disapproved of her costume for they concluded her male attire was not acceptable. McCleave questioned why her male costume would have raised such an objection, as cross-dressing was common practise in *opera seria*.[345] The public's reaction has been attributed by scholars to the contemporary perception of Sallé's lifestyle, rumoured as being independent and somewhat dubious.[346] However, this rejection could also be attributed to the fact Handel had re-used the dream sequences from *Ariodante*, which apparently the public deemed unacceptable as we have noticed previously.

For the conclusion of Act II, Alcina calls for vengeance for Ruggiero's unfaithfulness, yet the powers of darkness fail to reply. She quickly exits the stage, and the *ballo* commences; at this point, Handel inserted his dream sequences from *Ariodante*, which apparently was not his original intention. McCleave suggests according to the conducting score of *Alcina* the dances were a hasty addition; several sections of the manuscript are blank, implying Handel had planned to compose new dances, but there was insufficient time to accomplish this task.[347] McCleave also argues against Serauky's theory that Cupid's dance was possibly performed in Act II, stating that this claim cannot be substantiated, and alternatively suggested the dance could have taken place in Act I.[348] While McCleave's statement may be accurate, the possibility still remains that Cupid's dance was incorporated into the Act II pantomime sequence, which we should not overlook; Cupid may

---

[344] See "Le Pour et Contre," Paris [June?] 1735 in Deutsch, pp. 390–391.

[345] McCleave, *Dance in Handel's Operas*, p. 249–250.

[346] Ibid. p. 263.

[347] Ibid.

[348] Ibid. p. 267–268.

have entered during the *Entreé des songes agréables* while the dancers for the *Entreé des songes funestes* could have allegorically represented the demons summoned by Alcina. The battle that follows in *Le combat des Songes funestes et agréables* may have symbolically represented Alcina's emotional conflict between love and hate, and her desire for vengeance caused by the unfaithful love of Ruggiero. Therefore, the possibility still exists that Sallé danced in the dream sequences for *Alcina*, apparently rejected by the public previously in *Ariodante*, and this may account for the public's unwarranted rejection of her male attire. Yet, this was a singular aspect of the public's resistance; not only did their disapproval rest upon her costume, but apparently her dancing performance was also rejected. She had suddenly become so unpopular the audience hissed during one of her last appearances in *Alcina*; and hence 1734–35 was to be her final season at Covent Garden.[349]

Handel's use of dance, i.e. the pantomime-style sequence integrated with the drama, did not achieve the success he had anticipated. For instance, the majority of the dances from *Alcina* were printed in the sixth edition of *The Ladies' Banquet* (1735) with the exception of the Act II dream sequences and the entreé of Act III.[350] Evidently, the public favoured the dances from *Alcina* relating to contemporary popular theatrical and ballroom styles for these forms were widely published.[351] Despite the relative success *Alcina* achieved in contrast to *Ariodante*, the article from *Le Pour et Contre* dated May 1735 quoted previously appears to be more objective regarding audience turnout. Notably Handel was experiencing difficulty in attracting a full house; perhaps the more enthusiastic reception of *Alcina* influenced his decision to continue the production until July in the hope of recouping his severe losses — it was estimated Handel had already lost approximately 9,000

---

[349] See Deutsch, pp. 391–392.
[350] McCleave, *Dance in Handel's Operas*, p. 275.
[351] Ibid.

pounds.[352]

Despite these daunting circumstances, Handel continued to compound his difficulties while defending his music. Deutsch quoted Burney regarding an argument Handel engaged in with his lead castrato, Giovanni Carestini; apparently, Carestini had refused to sing the aria "Verdi prati" in *Alcina*, and Handel threatened to withhold his salary if he remained persistent in his refusal.[353] We may conclude Handel's insistence was correct for the aria was successful, yet Handel would once again suffer for his autocratic behaviour. Carestini departed London for Venice in July 1735 at the conclusion of the opera season, and when he returned to London in 1739–40, he never again performed for Handel.[354]

This incident concerning Carestini, and the lack of public interest in pantomime/dramatic dance combined with the sudden unpopularity of Sallé must have caused Handel to hesitate and take stock of his present predicament. The dissension between the two opera companies had not diminished as we observe in a letter written by Mrs. Pendarves to Swift dated May 16th, 1735.[355] Evidently, Handel decided to withdraw from opera production for the season of 1735–36; on October the 26th, 1735 an article printed in the *Evening Post* announced Handel would only produce oratorios and concerts of music that winter.[356] We observe that Lord Hervey, in a letter to Mrs. Charlotte Digby on November 25th, 1735, called Handel "a fool" for refusing to compose.[357] Hence we may conclude there is reason to believe Handel decided on a slight retreat from opera production as a tactical measure, and wished to bide his time.

Lord Hervey in the same letter relates how Handel attended

---

[352] Deutsch, p. 390.
[353] Ibid. p. 386. Quoting Burney, p. 24.
[354] Ibid. p. 392.
[355] Ibid. p. 390.
[356] Ibid. p. 395.
[357] Ibid. pp. 395–396.

an opera by Francesco Veracini at the Haymarket, (an unsuccessful production), where he "sat in great eminence and great pride in the middle of the pit, and seemed in silent triumph to insult this poor dying Opera in its agonies .... " Was Handel on a reconnaissance mission and scouting out the present position of his rivals? We cannot help but be amused at the prospect!

Scholars may argue Handel did not intend to suspend opera production that season as he revived *Ariodante* in May of 1736, and produced *Atalanta* for the nuptial celebrations of the Prince and Princess of Wales. However, we must observe that Handel did not have *Atalanta* prepared in time for the event, [358] and as an alternative, he was obliged to revive *Ariodante*. In addition, an article printed in the *Old Whig*, April 15th, 1736, announced Handel had engaged his new singers from Italy specifically for the wedding entertainments, [359] and *The London Daily Post* on April 29th, 1736 reported that same information. [360] Hence, Handel did not engage performers for a typical opera season, and this supports the theory Handel had decided to refrain from producing new operas for 1735–36. Alternatively, he introduced his ode *Alexander's Feast* on the 19th of February, and continued to revive his oratorios; perhaps he had planned to recoup his losses with productions of English works, as it appears he had previously attempted with his earlier engagements at Oxford?

Returning to Handel's opera productions for this short season, apparently he experimented yet again with previous methods; for *Atalanta*, Handel incorporated pastoral imagery and reintroduced the practise of minimal set changes reminiscent of his first production of *Il Pastor Fido* (1711). Thomas Gray, in his correspondence with Walpole, described the sets on June 11th, 1736 as follows:

---

358   Ibid. p. 405.
359   Ibid. p. 404.
360   Ibid. p. 405.

{...}There are only four men and two women in it. The first is a common scene of a wood, and does not change at all till the end of the last act, when there appears the Temple of Hymen with illuminations; {...}
361

However, when the scene changed the effect must have been spectacular. Gray continues:

{...} there is a row of blue fires burning in order along the ascent to the temple; a fountain of fire spouts up out of the ground to the ceiling, and two more cross each other obliquely from the sides of the stage; on top is a wheel that whirls always about, and throws out a shower of gold-colour, silver, and blue fiery rain. {...}
362

In the *London Daily Post* for May 13th, 1736, this description of the last scene was published:

{...} The Fore-part of the Scene represented an Avenue to the temple of *Hymen*, adorn'd with Figures of several Heathen Deities. Next was a Triumphal Arch on Top of which were the Arms of their Royal Highnesses, over which was placed a Princely Coronet. Under the Arch was the Figure of *Fame*, on a Cloud, sounding the Praise of this Happy Pair. The Names *Fredericus* and *Augusta* appear'd above in transparent Characters.
Thro' the Arch was seen a Pediment, supporting the Feathers, in a Princely Coronet, the Royal Ensign of

---

361 Ibid. p. 410.
362 Ibid.

the Prince of Wales. At the farther end was a View of Hymen's temple, and the Wings were adorn'd with the Loves and Graces bearing Hymeneal Torches, and putting Fire to Incense in Urns, to be offer'd up upon this joyful Union.

The Opera concluded with A Grand Chorus, during which several beautiful Illuminations were display'd, which gave an uncommon Delight and Satisfaction. {...}[363]

Obviously, Handel did not intend to have dance performed in *Atalanta*; there is a gavotte in the Act III finale although evidence is not presented in any of the sources indicating it was intended for dancers.[364] Dance was not performed in the revival of *Ariodante* in that season, or *Alcina* in the next despite the fact the dance troupe remained available. [365] We may of course attribute this omission to Sallé's departure; McCleave observes that when Sallé returned to France, Handel concentrated primarily on choral forces and apparently discontinued the idea of integrating dance into the operas.[366] She therefore surmised, "Handel and Rich failed to exploit a possible turning point for the production of Italian opera seria in London."[367]

This conclusion, however, may not be entirely accurate; Handel did attempt to introduce opera with dance integral to the dramatic plot. Perhaps Handel had finally realised the English were not receptive to pantomime-style dance in opera, and had not "failed to exploit" this aspect at all; as we have observed, it may have been the inclusion of this style of dance which the public objected to in opera. While the scenery of *Atalanta* seems to have been accepted

---

[363] Ibid. p. 407.
[364] McCleave, *Dance in Handel's Operas*, p. 276.
[365] Ibid. p. 276.
[366] Ibid. p. 277.
[367] Ibid.

with measured tolerance, complaints continued to be voiced by others. Subsequently, the Earl of Shaftsbury may have advised Handel that English preferences had evolved, for on June 29th, 1736, Handel wrote to the Earl:

> {...} I am extremely obliged to Your Lordship for sending me that Part of My Lord Your Fathers Letter relating to Musick. His notions are very just. I am highly delighted with them, and can not enough admire 'em. {...}[368]

Smith relates the theory proposed by McGeary that Handel's letter to the Earl on June 29th, 1736, refers to the correspondence by the Earl's father to Pierre Coste concerning Raguenet's treatise (1702) on the superiority of Italian to French opera. In this correspondence to Coste, Smith states that:

> Shaftsbury makes three aesthetic recommendations for modern music theatre: less elaborate scenery; restoration of the chorus; and simpler recitative, nearer to normal speech. 'Machines and Decorations' are 'vulgar, miserable, barbarous'; they were directly responsible for the decline of the Roman theatre, hastening the decay of Roman liberty through the corruption of public taste, and they abet the decay of liberty wherever they are allowed to dominate the theatre at the expense of thought-provoking, instructive drama — wherever the appeal is to the eye rather than the ear. {...} Shaftsbury speaks of the opportunity which the Italians have, in opera, for 'restoring the antient Tragedy (the true Opera) with its Chorus, and all the Charms depending on that antient Plan and

---

[368] Deutsch, p. 412.

Method'; as a result 'the Opera will every day gain upon the other Theatre, and our best Tragedy at last melt into Opera, which Union will be a kind of reviving the antient Tragedy in all its noble Orders of Musick and continu'd Harmony.'[369]

As we have noted in Handel's letter, he was particularly pleased with the Earl's suggestions, and this may explain why he finally abandoned his attempts at introducing dance within his operas, including elaborate scenic display as with *Atalanta*. Shaftsbury Sr.'s call for less "barbarous decorations" and the proposed method of defending "instructive drama" by increasing the use of chorus was reinforcing the idea of oratorio.

It would appear these noted innovations, with the exception of his addition of choral forces, which Handel had introduced to his operas before and during his Covent Garden term, had finally ended. Handel continued to compose Italian opera, but not with the same interest in dance. We may speculate, if Handel's rivals had not produced *Ottone* in opposition to him, would he have introduced *Ariodante* at a later date and not surprise the audiences of the day with a style he had not yet prepared them for, also, if Handel had not re-used the *Ariodante* dream-dances in *Alcina*, would he have been more successful with this production? We may only surmise this is a possibility; however, in this instance it would appear that Handel may have been his own worst enemy.

The same observation may also appertain to his actions regarding the premiere of *Deborah* and the dismissal of Senesino; if he had refrained from his hasty reactions, the intense rivalry between him and the Opera of the Nobility may have been avoided. He had

---

[369] Smith, *Oratorios*, p. 66. Her source, Thomas McGeary, 'Shaftsbury, Handel, and Italian Opera,' *HJb* 32 (1986): pp. 99–104. For a reprint of Raguenet's treatise, see François Raguenet, 'A Comparison Between the French and Italian Music,' *The Musical Quaterly*, vol. XXXII, No. 3 (July, 1946).

fostered public antipathy with his decisions, and consequently, his operas were shunned; only a handful of his staunch supporters attended his productions. This enduring public disapproval, allied with the rivalry, would continue to impede the remainder of Handel's endeavours at Covent Garden. On May 15th, 1736, Benjamin Victor wrote to Matthew Dubourg:

> {...} The two opera houses are, neither of them, in a successful way; and it is the confirmed opinion that this winter will complete your friend *Handel's* destruction, as far as the loss of his money can destroy him. {...} As to the Operas, they must tumble, for the King's presence could hardly hold them up, and even that prop is denied them, for his majesty will not admit his royal ears to be tickled this season. As to music, it flourishes in this place more than ever, in subscription concerts and private parties, which must prejudice all operas and public entertainments.[370]

Consequently, Handel was deprived of many of his loyal supporters at this time as they obdurately attended other entertainments, and his rivals were also adversely affected. Rolli was feeling trapped in these hard times — he had planned to leave for Rome as he related in his despondent letter a year earlier to Riva in June of 1735:

> {...} I have always loved and esteemed him, [Monsignior Passionei] and he has also loved me; thus I should like to keep him, as much as one can keep as friend a priest who is going to be a Cardinal just when I hope to go back and retire near Rome; because I am appallingly tired of this mud, smoke, and blasted eternal

---

[370] Deutsch, p. 409.

fog; where it is not easy for an honest and able foreigner to make even a modest living, and where it is necessary to spend enormous sums to live even decently and not get into debt, and to be obliged to play the politician for one's own safety, and as a result to cut a miserable figure. What a difficult Enigma! You don't know what it is like, for if you did, you would also know that a poor figure I cut on all sides.[371]

Rolli had corresponded with Riva sometime in 1736 requesting that he use his influence to obtain for him the appointment as Zeno's successor at the Emperor's court, or alternatively secure a position for him with the Duke of Modena who was Riva's patron.[372]   However, Metastasio received the appointment as Zeno's successor, therefore Rolli had no option but to remain in England. Dorris notes this period of Rolli's career was particularly disheartening, for his close circle of friends and supporters had been gradually diminishing.   Riva had been promoted to Vienna in 1729, Rolli's brother left in 1732, and Bononcini had departed England in disgrace in 1734 for pirating a work and claiming it as his own.[373] In the spring of 1736, Senesino and Cuzzoni departed for Italy, while Rolli and Farinelli remained to sustain and shoulder the heavy burden of the Opera of the Nobility, which would not last for long.[374]

---

[371] Dorris, *Italian Circle*, p. 153.

[372] Ibid.

[373] Ibid. p. 154. See also p. 100. Dorris observed, "By the time of the triumph of the Italians with the Opera of the Nobility, unfortunately, Bononcini was in disgrace and repute for having deceitfully plagiarized a madrigal by Lotti at the concerts of the Academy of Ancient Music (1732), upon which he quarrelled with his patrons, and quit the country the next year." Dorris must have implied the next season rather than the next year as he states the date of Bononcini's departure as 1734.

[374] Ibid.

Benjamin Victor in his aforementioned letter of May 15th, 1736 observed that the famous Farinelli was singing to "empty benches." Of notable interest, his letter intimates that the public created its own entertainment and refrained from attending the opera productions, which is reminiscent of the "Handel/Walpole" report stating that the public boycotted *Deborah* in 1733 by arranging their own amusements. Apparently, these tensions continued into the 1736–37 season. Mr. Pennington wrote this account to Miss Collingwood on the 19th of February 1737:

> {...} Partys run high in musick, as when you shone among us. Mr. Handel has not due honour done him, and I am excessively angry about it, which you know is of vast consequence.[375]

Circumstances must have drastically deteriorated when the Opera of the Nobility offered comic interludes that season, (which incidentally was contrary to Zeno's Arcadian ideology), perhaps as an attempt to attract audiences and fill the benches. Apparently, Rolli must have reached the end of his tether and was forced to abandon his Arcadian ambitions, for he arranged the opera *Sabrina* in the last season, which was based on Milton's *Comus*, and included comic interludes. (See Appendix Four.) Similar to his plan when Carestini departed from London, Handel once again threatened he would not compose any more (operas?) according to a letter by Miss Ann Granville in March of 1737:

> Music is certainly a pleasure that may be reckoned intellectual, and we shall *never again* have it in the perfection it is this year, because Mr. Handel *will not compose any more!* Oratorios begin next week, to my great joy, for they are the highest entertainment to

---

[375] Deutsch, p. 426.

me.[376]

However, Handel's health was gradually declining; it was reported in April he was suffering from rheumatism, and as a result, he did not direct his operas of *Dido* on April 13th, or *Berenice* on 18th of May.[377] By May it was realised Handel had a "Paraletick Disorder" which was more severe than previous reports indicated.[378] Finally, he travelled to Aix-la-Chapelle for the vapour-baths in the hope of a recovery; *Berenice* was Handel's final new opera for this particular period at Covent Garden, and the last time Conti and Strada would perform in London.[379] The Opera of the Nobility was forced to accept their premature demise on the 11th of June 1737.[380] Farinelli had fallen ill, and the final night of the season was cancelled; he subsequently departed for Italy with the composer Porpora following suit.[381]

We again observe Italian opera ardently criticised in an article from the *Craftsman* on June 4th, 1737:

> {...} however, if *this Bill* [for restraining the Liberty of the Stage] must pass ... I hope our *Italian Opera's* will fall the first Sacrifice, as they not only carry great Sums of Money out of the Kingdom, but soften and enervate the Minds of the People. It is observable of the *antient Romans*, that they did not admit of any *effeminate Musick*, *Singing* or *Dancing*, upon their Stage, till *Luxury* had corrupted their Morals, and the Loss of *Liberty* follow'd soon after. If therefore it should be thought necessary to lay any further Restraint

---

[376] Ibid. p. 428.
[377] Ibid. pp. 432–433.
[378] Ibid. p. 434.
[379] Ibid. p. 435.
[380] Ibid. p. 437.
[381] Ibid.

upon the *most useful Sort of dramatical Entertainments*, the *worst* ought certainly to receive no Encouragement.[382]

Decisively, this desperate situation had its roots planted with the rivalry between Handel and those influenced by Rolli's circle; their two companies had in effect created a stalemate. Those who were irate with Handel concerning the *Deborah* premiere were wearied by the Opera of the Nobility productions,[383] yet many repeatedly refused to attend Handel's operas despite the general preference for his music, including nights when there were no other public entertainments available.[384] The rival opera companies needed to cooperate and pool their resources if they were to produce any successful operas as Benjamin Victor reflected, "We are not without hopes of Senesino's return to England, and once more seeing him in his most advantageous light, *singing Handel's compositions.*"[385] Hence, Handel's rivalry and his reactions to Rolli's supporters, in conjunction with their retaliations, had disrupted the production of *opera seria* in London — impeding any progress that was attempted. We are not surprised these opera ventures did not survive under these circumstances.

In summation of documents researched, information gathered, discoveries and the philosophical reconstruction of the chain of events, I conclude Handel's relocation to Covent Garden in 1734 and his subsequent difficulties were linked to his problems with Rolli and his Arcadian circle which originated before and during the formation of the Royal Academy. From the days of the Royal Academy continuing on to the Second Academy, it appears

---

[382] Ibid. p. 436.

[383] See Lord Hervey's letter dated 1735 and Mrs. Pendarve's letter dated 1736 in Deutsch, pp. 395, 418.

[384] Ibid. p. 384.

[385] Ibid. p. 409.

Handel concluded his position and his artistic right to oversee and protect the integrity of his works was threatened by those who influenced his patrons. The nobility also played their part; once before, Handel's patrons had practically assured him he would be head composer of the Royal Academy. However, they apparently reneged on this agreement when factions supporting Bononcini and Amadei developed. Subsequently, the collaborative contest with regard to *Muzio Scevola* had temporarily settled the problem, however, Handel continued to encounter aggravation from Rolli and his supporters.

In the Second Academy, the directors had agreed to grant Handel his freedom as head composer and the authority to elect those with whom he wished to work. Evidently, the directors had yet again broken their agreement when Bononcini was allowed to produce his serenata, and to Handel, this was the final insult. If tensions, suspicions, and mistrust had not escalated over the years, Handel may not have reacted as hastily concerning the premiere of *Deborah* and the dismissal of Senesino. His decision to assert his authority and usurp total control for his last season at the Haymarket may have precipitated the formation of the Opera of the Nobility company and ultimately effected his relocation to Covent Garden. However, his problems continued to escalate, in an almost domino-like effect, which also influenced his innovations at Covent Garden. Finally, the rivalry between the two companies resulted in a stalemate; the rival factions had weakened the position of Italian opera in London, facilitating the progression of oratorio.

Could the circumstances that created the rivalry and this unstable situation have been prevented? All the factions involved, i.e. the directors, Handel, Rolli and his group, contributed towards these catastrophic events that ultimately affected the opera culture of London. Evidently, the survival of the Royal Academy depended on the cooperation of those who were actively involved with the company, yet when these individual factions stubbornly defended their personal ideologies, it proved impossible to work harmoniously and the success of the company was limited. Perchance if the nobility complied with the established understanding and declared general policy for the production of opera as stated in the Subscriber's Prospectus during the formation of the Royal Academy, a regulated, orderly business decorum may have been achieved. Instead, they became divided in their support between Handel and the Arcadians, which subsequently caused numerous altercations. This unfortunate situation created tensions and uncertainties with the production of Italian opera in London, with far reaching effects into the 1730s and beyond. This turbulent state may have been averted if all the parties concerned had diplomatically ignored their personal differences and had adopted a positive approach for the mutual success of opera in London.

Chapter 5

An Addendum: Independence and Expectations

Having considered Handel's tumultuous opera career and his first term at Covent Garden in the 1730s, perhaps we may dare to suggest he was one of the foremost pioneers in establishing autonomy within the traditional system of music patronage, notwithstanding his efforts to become an independent impresario often proved disappointing. Handel was not content to work as an "insignificant" composer, which was the general perception of their status within the traditional process of opera composition in Italy. Obviously, the appointment of House Composer at the Royal Academy of London was more appealing, as this position allowed him more control over his works and offered the opportunity to promote the status of his role as the musical creator of his productions, which he ardently defended. In addition, he would not be placed under the direct patronage, nor be restricted by any one member of the aristocracy in that institution, as the Royal Academy operated as a public subscription venture. However, he eventually concluded that his subordinate position to the directors and their managerial pressures interfered with his artistic endeavours, and he rebelled to this situation by usurping the role of impresario in the Second Academy. It would appear he finally achieved relative managerial freedom while working with Rich at Covent Garden. Handel's yearning for independence from the traditional chains of patronage and his persistence in monitoring his productions resulted with unique developments concerning Baroque *opera seria*; however, paradoxically his personal obsession to obtain complete artistic freedom generated disastrous side-affects that eventually impeded the progress of opera in London. With the exception of his artistic temperament, an interesting question comes to our attention; why was Handel so insistent on maintaining his independence and complete control over the production of his operas? Perhaps the answer lies within Handel's formative years, a time when important psychological patterns and natural characteristics regarding personality take shape.

Hogwood made an interesting observation when he stated, "The childhoods of the great tend to be forced into one of two patterns — angel or martyr. Handel's biographers have traditionally taken the later stance …".[386] This martyrdom for the sake of music has been attributed to Mainwaring's account in which he relates Georg Händel Sr. sternly opposed an "undignified" occupation in music for his son as he wished him to pursue a career in civil law — musical instruments therefore became prohibited objects in their home, and Handel was never permitted to make social visits where musical instruments were available. Handel eventually defied his father's authority; he secretly smuggled a small clavichord into the attic and taught himself how to play with prodigious success when the household was asleep. Although Mainwaring's biography is faulty concerning the chronology of Handel's youth, we may still presume these incidents were not complete fiction, as Mainwaring relied on Handel's amanuensis, John Christopher Smith, as his principal source of information. Could this authoritarian, strict regime enforced by Handel's father in their home, as these anecdotes display, have fostered a rebellious and autocratic disposition in his son? By briefly examining the biography of Handel's father as related by Hogwood, perhaps we may discover his reasons for opposing music as a vocation for Handel.

Georg Händel Sr.[387] was the fifth son born to a coppersmith named Valentin Händel in 1622, a staunch Lutheran family. When his father died in 1636, Georg was apprenticed to a surgeon–barber

---

[386] Hogwood, *Handel*, p. 12.

[387] This history of Handel's father is derived from Hogwood's account. See *Handel*, pp. 11–12.

at the age of fourteen; at that time, these occupations were a combined trade. Upon the death of his second trade-master, Christoph Oettinger, Handel Sr. married Oettinger's wife, with whom he subsequently had two children. This marriage of convenience boded well for Georg as he assumed the ownership of the business and was thereby appointed surgeon and *valet de chamber* to Duke Augustus of Saxony. However, the Treaty of Westphalia that signalled the end of the Thirty Years War in 1648 eventually affected his appointment. It had been agreed, as a condition of this peace treaty, that upon the death of Duke Augustus, the town of Halle would come under the jurisdiction of Prussia. Therefore, when Augustus died in 1680, the centre of power transferred to the Brandenburgs in Berlin, and Georg subsequently found himself employed within the new court of the Duke of Weissenfels, nearly twenty miles from Halle. In 1682, when he reached the age of sixty, his wife died, and shortly after he remarried. Georg's second wife was the thirty-two year old daughter of a pastor, and therefore nearly thirty years his junior. Their first son died at birth, and their second son, Handel, was born on the 23rd of February 1685; they also had two daughters, Dorothea Sophia and Johanna Christiana.

As observed previously, Mainwaring's biography presents Georg Handel Sr. as a father who was a strict disciplinarian and authoritarian in nature. We also perceive Mainwaring attempted to display Georg's belief in adhering to domestic and professional protocol dictated by his era through the account of Georg's journey to Weissenfels when Handel was a young boy. According to Mainwaring, Georg Sr. initially refused his son the opportunity to travel with him on that particular journey as it was related to his professional duties, despite Handel's entreaties to visit his half-brother, Karl, whom he had never met, and incidentally, who was employed by the Duke of Weissenfels. Mainwaring stated that Georg "thought one of his age a very improper companion when he was going to the court of a Prince, and to attend the duties of his profession."[388] Hence, we may assume Georg upheld the opinion that children should be kept in their place despite Handel's desire to meet his half-brother.

However, Handel was determined to travel to Weissenfels, and set out on foot after his father's carriage, notwithstanding that the journey to Weissenfels was nearly twenty miles! Fortunately for Handel, the carriage had not travelled far when his father saw him and relented; Handel had therefore achieved his aim and travelled with his father to Weissenfels despite his father's convictions regarding professional protocol.

A very important question to consider: why did Georg Sr. disapprove of music as a career for Handel? Mainwaring observed he did not object to it as a pastime, for he deemed it an "elegant art and a fine amusement."[389] In addition, Georg apparently owned musical instruments at one time for Mainwaring states Handel "had made some progress before Music had been prohibited," i.e. before Handel was compelled to embark on nightly undercover missions to the attic.[390] Georg explained to the Duke of Weissenfels the reasons for his objections, stating that he considered music an undignified occupation, as it had "for its object nothing better than mere pleasure and entertainment." [391] This suggests religious and moral scruples with possible origins in Lutheran Pietism were partially responsible. Fortunately for Handel, (and the history of music!) the Duke advised Georg not to restrict his son in his desire to learn music, as he observed the boy was exceptionally talented during his stay at Weissenfels.

It may also be debated if Georg objected to the fact his son would have traditionally been considered a servant in that

---

[388] Mainwaring, pp. 2–3. Mainwaring states Handel was seven at this time, while Hogwood says a probable date for this incident would be 1696 when Handel was eleven. Hogwood, *Handel*, p. 13.

[389] Mainwaring, p. 10.

[390] Ibid. p. 5.

[391] Ibid. pp. 11–12.

occupation, as musicians were not yet fully emancipated "artistic geniuses" worthy of "stellar" fame, awe and admiration with the option to embark on public careers. However, we may observe that he and other members of his family were under appointment to the nobility, and he regarded them with great respect. For instance, he immediately followed the Duke's advice despite his reluctance and allowed Handel to fulfil his ambitions; therefore, this aspect of working for the nobility may not have been his sole reason for concern.

Perhaps the *lack of independence* associated with this career in having to rely considerably on the private patronage of the nobility or the church was the paramount factor that concerned his father. As previously observed, Georg experienced first hand the difficulties that may occur with an occupation tied to the fortunes of the aristocracy. Hogwood also observed that Georg's decision was the natural reaction of an elderly father who was worried for his son's future:

> In a declining township with its court patronage now removed and the effects of the Thirty Years Was still evident in its poverty and stricken economy, a preoccupation with music could be the start of a disastrous career, particularly if the young boy were not talented.[392]

As a concerned father, Georg desired a secure profession for his son where he could remain the master of his own destiny. The career he had chosen in civil law was not only respectable, it was a vocation in life where Handel could retain a measure of freedom; he would not be completely dependant on the whims of the nobility, nor be restricted to the disciplined regimes associated with church employment. Supporting this perception is the subsequent incident

---

[392] Hogwood, *Handel*, p. 12.

that occurred when Georg brought Handel to Berlin for cultural advancement in music.

Hogwood confirms this journey must have occurred in 1697 before Georg Sr. died on February 11th, 1697.[393] Mainwaring relates that Handel had "a friend and relation" at the court of Berlin and states:

> ... the little stranger {Handel} had not been long at court before his abilities became known to the King, {the Elector}, who frequently sent for him, and made him large presents. Indeed his Majesty, convinc'd of his singular endowments, and unwilling to lose the opportunity of patronizing so rare a genius, had conceived a design of cultivating it as his own expense. His intention was to send him to Italy, where he might be formed under the best masters, and have opportunities of hearing and seeing all that excellent kind. As soon as it was intimated to HANDEL's friends (for he was yet too young to determine for himself) they deliberated what answer it would be proper to return, in case this scheme should be proposed in form. {...} Others, who better understood the temper and spirit of the court of Berlin, thought this a matter of nice speculation, and cautious debate. For they well knew, that if he once engag'd in the King's service, he must remain in it, whether he liked it or not; that if he continued to please, it would be a reason for not parting with him; and that if he happened to displease, his ruin would be the certain consequence. To accept an offer of this nature, was the same thing as to enter into a formal engagement, but how to refuse it was still the difficulty. At length it was

---

[393] Ibid. p. 16.

resolved that some excuse must be found. It was not long before the King caused his intentions to be signified, and the answer was, that the Doctor {Georg Sr.} would always retain the profoundest sense of the honour done to him by the notice which his Majesty had been graciously pleased to take of his son; but as he himself was now grown old, and could not expect to have him long with him, he humbly hoped the King would forgive his desire to decline the offer which had been made him by order of his Majesty.

I am not able to inform the reader how this answer was relished by the King, whom we may suppose not much accustomed to refusals, especially of this sort. Such an incident made it improper for HANDEL to stay much longer at the court of Berlin, where the more his abilities should be known and commended, the more some persons would be apt to sift and scrutinize the motives of his father's conduct.[394]

Undoubtedly, this incident in Berlin which occurred just before his twelfth birthday, a this susceptible age, left a marked impression on Handel's memory — particularly when his father's prophecy concerning his advancement in years was fulfilled shortly thereafter. It is not surprising his objective to remain autonomous became a major factor during the remainder of Handel's life, as Mainwaring relates.[395] Handel's independent streak was not fostered by a rebellious nature, but sprang from his filial loyalty to the memory of his father. We may deduce that the stories concerning Handel's ingenuity in concealing a secret clavichord in the attic, and his plan to journey on foot behind his father's carriage to the court of Weissenfels were acts of strong determination; he acted upon

---

[394] Mainwaring, pp. 22–25.
[395] Ibid. p. 28.

compelling instincts to fulfil personal ambitions, but nothing more.

If Handel truly wished to be rebellious, he had the opportunity after his father's death; however, he enrolled at the new university of Halle on 10th of February 1702. We are not aware which faculty he was affiliated with, however we may surmise he attempted, without success, to follow the career plans his father had envisioned for him, as Mainwaring states, "... the Civil Law could have had no share of his attention."[396] He finally abandoned the university nearly a year later; a career in law did not appeal to him, and the operas of Hamburg became an irresistible attraction — employed by Reinhard Keiser in an opera house dependant upon public support, Handel first experienced the life of an impresario-composer. It would be natural for Handel to feel some portion of guilt for failing to fulfil his father's wishes, despite his musical inclinations; possibly a desire to honour his loyalty to his father while remaining true to his artistic temperament created a psychological conflict that gravely affected Handel throughout his career. Perchance he perceived the only possible solution would be to prove that he could embark on the career of a musician and remain independent, never condescending to the level of a servant, and thereby honour the memory of his father. This would explain his ambition to acquire positions of authority, and his subsequent attempts to elevate his status as composer.

Evidence supporting this theory is manifested in Handel's early career. According to John Mattheson, Handel on two occasions assumed the position as orchestra-leader[*] at the opera house in Hamburg:

> Handel came to Hamburg in the summer of 1703, rich only in ability and goodwill. {...} At first he played ripieno violin in the opera orchestra, and

---

[396] Ibid. p.17.

[*] In Baroque times, the leader of the orchestra conducted from the harpsichord.

behaved as if he could not count to five, being naturally inclined to dry humour. ... But once the harpsichord player failed to appear he allowed himself to be persuaded to take his place, and showed himself a man — a thing no one had before suspected, save I alone.[397]

The second occurrence of Handel's self-promotion precipitated the famous duel between the two friends:

> On 5 December [1704] ... when my third opera, *Cleopatra*, was being performed, with Handel at the harpsichord, a misunderstanding arose: such a thing is nothing new with young people who strive after honour with all their power and very little consideration. I, as composer, directed, and at the same time sang the part of Antonius, who, about half-an-hour before the end of the play, commits suicide. Now until that occasion I had been accustomed, after this section, to go into the orchestra and accompany the rest myself: which unquestionably the author can do better than anyone else; this time, however, Handel refused to give up his place. Incited by several people who were present, we fought a duel at the exit of the Opera House, in the open market place and with a crowd of onlookers. Things might have passed off very unfortunately for both of us, had God's guidance not graciously ordained that my blade, thrusting against the broad, metal coat-button of my opponent, should be shattered. No harm came of the affair, {...} we were soon reconciled again. {...}[398]

---

[397] Mattheson, *Grundlage einer Ehren-Pforte*, (Hamburg 1740, ed. M. Schneider, Berlin 1910, repr. 1969), in Hogwood, *Handel* p. 23.
[398] Mattheson, ibid, in Hogwood, *Handel*, p. 24. Mainwaring

We may observe, Handel did not wish to waste any time in his endeavour to obtain a position of notable status in the opera house of Hamburg; in one year, Handel was afforded the opportunity to compose two operas, *Almira* and *Nero,* for the opera house in 1705.

In addition, Handel continued to avoid compromising situations; undoubtedly the consternation that resulted from the gracious offer of the Elector of Berlin when he was a young boy of twelve was forever etched in his memory. We note his reservations in accepting assistance from the aristocrats for he insulted Prince Ferdinand de' Medici as a desperate ploy to maintain his independence despite his ardent wish to travel to Italy. The Prince offered him an opportunity to visit that Elysium of music, but according to Mainwaring, Handel planned to travel by private means and on his own initiative:

> The Prince was a great lover of the art for which his country is so renowned. {...} The Prince would often lament that Handel was not acquainted with those {i.e. composers, singers and performers}, of Italy; shewed him a large collection of Italian Music; and was very desirous he should return with him to Florence. Handel plainly confessed that he could see nothing in the Music which answered the high character his Highness had given it. On the contrary, he thought it so very indifferent, that the Singers, he said, must be angels to recommend it. The Prince smiled at the severity of his censure, and added, that there needed

---

confuses Handel's age, and recounts an obviously embellished version where Mattheson attacked Handel without any warning, who nevertheless escaped his brush with death by the musical score of the opera that he had carried within his coat. Mainwaring, p. 35.

nothing but a journey to Italy to reconcile him to the style and taste which prevailed there. He assured him that there was no country in which a young proficient could spend his time to so much advantage; or in which every branch of his profession was cultivated with so much care. Handel replied, that if were so, he was much at a loss to conceive how such great culture should be followed by so little fruit. However, what his Highness had told him, and what he had before heard of the fame of the Italians, would certainly induce him to undertake the journey he had been pleased to recommend, the moment it should be convenient. The Prince then intimated, that if he chose to return with him, no conveniences should be wanting. Handel, without intending to accept of the favour designed him, expressed his sense of the honour done him. For he resolved to go to Italy on his own bottom, as soon as he could make a purse for that occasion. This noble spirit of independency, which possessed him almost from his childhood, was never to forsake him, not even in the most distressful seasons of his life.[399]

In addition, he also displayed his reluctance in becoming employed full-time with ecclesiastical institutions. Handel held a position at the Calvinist Cathedral of Halle for one year while he attended the university, and this was the only traditional music post he held in Germany. We must assume this experience was responsible for deterring him from accepting a permanent position in the ecclesiastical world; although he had often played the organ in the cathedral on a substitute basis, his new duties were more demanding, as he was required:

---

[399] Mainwaring, pp. 39–41.

205

... to play the organ fittingly at Divine Service, and for this purpose to prelude on the prescribed Psalms and Spiritual Songs, and to have due care to whatever might be needful to the support of beautiful harmony, to take heed to this end, that he be always in Church in good time and before the pealing of the bell ceases, and no less take good care of the preservation of the organ and whatever appertains to the same.[400]

His experiences in Italy with respect to the various attempts to covert him to Catholicism as Mainwaring relates, and the fact that the Pope banned opera in Rome, may have fuelled his determination to remain independent — free from the dictates associated with aristocratic and ecclesiastical circles. We are not surprised Handel finally decided to settle in London; Percy M. Young observed that:

By birth he {Handel} was a member of this stratum of society {the middle classes}, and he chose to live in a city where it was possible for his peers to retain both spiritual and economic independence. {...} This mutual-improvement society, with its array of peers and peeresses, justices and civil servants, merchants and artists, natives and aliens, was unique in the Europe of those days {...}, and the conclusion may be drawn that the possibilities of wide camaraderie were instrumental in engaging Handel's affection for the English. Pepusch, it will be remembered, felt very much as Handel did about residence here. He had left Germany through hatred of, and evidence of, tyranny. Hawkins reported Handel's observation that in England it was possible for a man to hold to whatever religious views he pleased without fear of molestation. This is a

---

[400] 'Appointment of the organist, Hendel', 13th March 1702, records of Halle Cathedral, in Hogwood, *Handel*, p. 21.

statement of significance.[401]

Hence, Handel would agree to assume a position upon certain conditions whereby he was guaranteed significant freedom — many of his positions were "congenial arrangements" where he was a guest composer rather than a composer-in-residence, as Hogwood describes Handel's employment with Cardinal Ruspoli in Italy, and Burlington and Chandos in England.[402] Handel always aspired to maintain a position of authority, thereby making it possible for him to elevate his status as a musician. Therefore, we are not surprised to observe that Handel felt compelled to defend his position of authority at the Haymarket, and autocratically assumed the role of impresario in the Second Academy and at Covent Garden.

Ironically, there are also indications that the rivalry that brought forth bitter consequences at the Royal Academy partially originated from Handel's early years in Germany. Mainwaring related Handel first encountered Bononcini and Attilio Ariosti in Berlin (1698); however, Hogwood observed that Mainwaring's,

> {...} mention of a meeting with the composers {...} sets the date after Georg Händel's death, since Ariosti arrived in Berlin only later in 1697, and Bononcini not until 1702. Mainwaring's account may be a conflation of more than one visit; alternatively Handel may have met the two Italians during his time in Hamburg.[403]

Therefore, it is logical to assume that Handel may have been introduced to them when he was eighteen. Obviously, there was no animosity between Handel and Ariosti; Mainwaring relates Ariosti

---

[401] Percy M. Young, 'Handel the Man', in *Handel: A Symposium*, p. 10.
[402] Hogwood, *Handel*, p. 37.
[403] Hogwood, *Handel*, p.16.

enjoyed Handel's harpsichord performances, and had great admiration for this musical genius, a feeling that was cordially returned, for Handel never forgot Ariosti's generosity to him.[404] Apparently, Handel always repaid kindnesses shown to him with the same affection; it is not surprising that there is no indication of major rivalry between Ariosti and Handel at the Haymarket. Mainwaring described Ariosti as a "sweet tempered" and modest man,[405] who apparently was content with his own position at the Haymarket, for as Dean and Knap surmised, he did not find it necessary to satisfy any particular need for control concerning his operas.[406] Perhaps he was pleased to see "his" previously adopted prodigy of the harpsichord assume a position of authority and respect.

In contrast, it is apparent Handel believed he had every reason to be mistrustful of Bononcini at the Haymarket because of a previous insulting experience he had with him in Germany. According to Mainwaring, Bononcini, who believed this young prodigy was stealing the limelight from him, challenged Handel. Bononcini composed a particularly complicated cantata in the "chromatic style, difficult in every respect" in an attempt to test the exaggerated accounts of his young rival; we may assume he presented this piece to Handel while attending a social gathering where he would be obliged to perform it sight unseen for the amusement of those who were present. However, Bononcini was forced to acknowledge Handel's technical skill and musical ability when he performed the work in question to perfection without the necessity to practise.[407] If this account is true, no doubt the young, fiery prodigy was personally insulted with this unexpected trap to ridicule him and his skill if he had failed, in addition to the fact that Bononcini considered him no more than a mere child. Obviously,

---

[404] Ibid, p. 21.
[405] Ibid, p. 20.
[406] Dean and Knapp, *Handel's Opera's*, f. 15, p. 17.
[407] Mainwaring, pp.19–20.

this anecdote bears the stamp of authenticity for it is reasonable to assume that very few people in later times other than Handel would have remembered the details concerning the nature of the piece described as "chromatic". If Handel could not set aside a grudge, it is presumable Bononcini did not forget his resentment; Mainwaring described Bononcini as a man fond of applause and therefore we may deduce he was as eager as Handel to assume notable positions, hence, the manifestation of their rivalry at the Royal Academy is comprehensible.

After considering Handel's reactions, and the possibility they may have stemmed from a psychological need to prove his independence as a musician and composer, our attentions inevitably turn to Paolo Rolli, his Arcadian supporters, and their exasperation with the management and the production of opera in London. In contrast, we may perceive they entertained great expectations with regard to the Royal Academy and the Opera of the Nobility, which eventually resulted in complete disappointment.

The source of their initial expectations may be traced to the public Teatro Capranica in Rome, originally a private theatre in the palace of Cardinal Domenico Capranica during the fifteenth century.[408] However, the Teatro Capranica was first opened as a public venture by his cousins Pompeo and Federico (Alveri) Capranica in 1694. Due to the perceived immoral aspect of opera, the doors were closed in 1698 by order of Pope Innocent XII; however, in the years 1711–24 it was reopened and two *drammi per musica* were produced each carnival season, as was customary for the public opera houses of that era. Strohm remarks this was a unique period in the history of the Teatro Capranica:

{...} we could identify this period as that of

---

[408]   This information concerning the Teatro Capranica is based on Strohm's essay 'A context for Griselda: the Teatro Capranica in Rome, 1711-1724, in *Dramma per Musica*, pp. 33–60.

'Arcadian opera before Metastasio'. Members of the Accademia dell'Arcadia were indeed connected with the Teatro Capranica more than perhaps with any other public venture in Rome. {...} This short period was indeed the only episode in Roman opera history when Arcadians influenced a public opera house.[409]

Of particular interest to us are the years 1715–17; there is a strong possibility that the formation of the Royal Academy was modelled upon the Teatro Capranica, as it was the only public theatre in Rome producing opera seria at that time. It is probable that members of the British aristocracy who made the Grand Tour of Italy those seasons would have attended public opera in Rome — undoubtedly they were influenced by their experience at the Teatro Capranica. We may identify at least three members of the nobility who must have attended: Lord Burlington, Lord Stair, and possibly the Earl of Pembroke.

We know that Lord Burlington visited Rome in 1715; however, the information relating the other two names, Stair and Pembroke, we obtain through documentation relating Rolli's invitation to England. Rolli directed the rehearsals at the Capranica Theatre in 1715, and later that same year he arrived in the British Isles. (Incidentally, Bononcini had moved to Rome that same year and co-produced *Astarto* with Rolli at the Capranica.) Dorris quotes Giambatista Tondini, the editor of Rolli's *Marziale in Albion*, who recounted that Rolli travelled to England with "Mylord Steers Sembuck," which obviously is a confused jumble of one or more factual names.[410] In addition, Dorris also mentions A. Salza's theory that the name "Sembuck" indicated the eighth Earl of Pembroke.[411]

---

[409] Ibid, p. 34.

[410] From Rolli, 'Marziale in Albion ... premesseve le memories della vita dell'autore compilate dall'ab. Giambatista Tondini ...' (Firenze, 1776) p. 4., in Dorris, Italian Circle, p. 133.

[411] From 'Note biografiche e bibliografiche intorno a Paolo Rolli',

However, Dorris observed an important letter written by Riva to Muratori dated January 31st, 1716 was neglected — this letter states unquestionably that Lord George Dalrymple Stair brought Rolli to England:

> There has just joined us from Rome, with the brother of the Lord Stair, the abate Rolli, a fine poet and marvellous improvisator, whom I knew in Rome, and whom we are both very happy to find here. [412]

Dorris therefore concluded that Lord Stair and the Earl of Pembroke were in Rome and both offered Rolli their patronage, thus accounting for Todini's confusion of the names.[413]

An intriguing observation, Strohm mentions Lindgren's theory that Lord Burlington actually brought Rolli to England based upon his study of the libretto of the revival of *Astarto* in 1720 at the Royal Academy; Burlington had attended the 1715 Capranica production and Rolli dedicated the London libretto to him.[414] However, Riva's letter above contradicts this theory; we must therefore, as an alternative, assume that Burlington encouraged Rolli and Bononcini with many alluring promises to come to England, which corresponds with Mainwaring's account that several parties wished to include Bononcini in the Royal Academy.

As the initial concept of a permanent opera company for London was gathering momentum in 1717-1719 when opera productions had ceased, it would be a logical assumption that their plans were influenced by the nobility who had travelled to Rome

---

Bolletino della Real Deputazione di Storia Patria per l'Umbria, XIX (1915). Fasc. I, n.47, p. 103. In Dorris, p. 133.

[412] From Vallese, *Paolo Rolli in Inghilterra*, (Milano, 1938), p. 7., in Dorris, p. 134.

[413] Dorris, p. 136.

[414] From L. Lindgren, A Bibliographic Scrutiny, pp.157–8, in Strohm, *Dramma per Musica*, pp. 47–48.

when the Capranica was the sole public theatre in 1715-1717. Elizabeth Gibson observed that the young directors who had made the Grand Tour were, "...perhaps impressed by the musical productions that they had seen abroad," and "...were ready to try to create something similar in London."[415] Incidentally, Lord Burlington, including many members of his social circle, and Lord Stair were active members in the Royal Academy. Hence, when the British nobility paid flattering attentions to Rolli and Bononcini, expressed their admiration for their opera productions when travelling in Italy, and intimated they wished to produce Italian opera in England, these two Italians may have been led to believe that the public subscription venture of the Royal Academy would reflect the Teatro Capranica in Rome, which as mentioned was the only theatre completely influenced by Arcadian idealism.

Rolli in particular may have entertained high expectations, as he was initially appointed Italian Secretary of the Royal Academy; therefore, he may have expected this new opera venture to flourish as a new Arcadian company if the nobility wished to emulate the public Capranica theatre and its productions. Their expectations may have been reinforced when Bononcini's *Astarto* was extremely successful in London. However, the management of the company did not follow the Arcadian conventions; we must not forget that the English realised pure Arcadian opera did not suit their cultural environment, thus we observe one instance where Rolli and Bononcini's expectations would be dashed.

In addition, we must also observe the Arcadians did not allow the composer assume a high status, which was reserved for the dramatists. Therefore, when the English decided to elect a House Composer for the Royal Academy, particularly when they considered Handel who supported English preferences regarding opera, we observe further grounds for Rolli's displeasure. According

---

[415] Elizabeth Gibson, *The Royal Academy of Music, 1719–1728: the Institution and its Directors*, (New York: Garland Publishing Inc., 1989), p. 52, in Taylor, *Italian Operagoing*, p. 73.

to Strohm:

> Some useful secondary functions of the public
> opera houses {in Rome} included that of the 'fall-back'
> opportunity: when artists and staff {i.e. of the private
> aristocratic establishments} were no longer needed, they
> could be hived off to the public theatre. [416]

Apparently, a Head Composer was not traditionally
appointed at the Capranica, as the availability of dramatists,
performers, and composers varied according to this patronage
system, thus Rolli and his supporters may have been annoyed with
this new system in London of employing a Head Composer and the
failure of operating a relatively "equal opportunity" venture.
Despite these disappointing results, apparently Rolli and Bononcini
attempted to remain in contact with the Teatro Capranica with their
operas *Crispo* and *Griselda* during the 1721–22 season at the
Haymarket. [417]

Obviously, the contentions at the Royal Academy included
Handel's determination to uphold his independence, and Rolli and
his supporters' defence of their expectations. No doubt, these two
aspirations unavoidably clashed; both may be compared to opposing
atmospheric fronts that immediately broke over the proceedings at
the Haymarket, thus creating a tornado of antagonism and rivalry.
Unfortunately, the opera culture of London could not weather the
storm that brewed, and the Royal Academy eventually became an
artistic disaster zone. We may observe Handel was more fortunate

---

[416] Strohm, *Dramma per Musica*, p. 36.
[417] *Crispo* and *Griselda* were first produced in 1721 at the Capranica.
Bononcini composed the music for *Crispo* and the libretto was written
by Gaetano Lemer, a friend of Rolli. Scarlatti originally composed the
music for *Griselda*, but Bononcini composed a new score for the
London revival, the text was by Zeno. See Strohm, *Dramma per
musica*, pp. 54–55.

in withstanding this hurricane through his ability to adapt, adopting the oratorio genre when the vogue for opera had failed; the expectations may have been optimistic, but independence obviously had its advantages.

Appendix One[418]

Aaron Hill's preface to the word book of Rinaldo (1711).

When I ventur'd on an Undertaking so hazardous as the Direction of OPERA's in their present Establishment, I resolv'd to spare no Pains or Cost, that might be requisite to make those Entertainments flourish in their proper Grandeur, that so at least it might not be my Fault if the Town should hereafter miss so noble a Diverson.

The Deficiencies I found, or thought I found, in such ITALIAN OPERA's as have hitherto been introduc'd among us were, *First*, That they have been compos'd for Tastes and Voices, different from those who were to sing and hear them on the *English* Stage; And *Secondly*, That wanting the Machines and Decorations, which bestow so great a beauty on their Appearance, they have been heard and seen to very considerable Disadvantage.

At once to remedy both these Misfortunes, I resolv'd to frame some Dramma, that, by different Incidents and Passions, might afford the Musick Scope to vary and display its Excellence, and fill the Eye with more delightful Prospects, so at once give Two Senses equal Pleasure.

I could not chuse a finer subject than the celebrated Story of *Rinaldo* and *Armida*, which has furnish'd OPERA's for every Stage and Tounge in *Europe*. I have, however, us'd a Poet's Privilege, and

---

418 Deutsch, pp. 32–33.

var'y from the Scheme of Tasso, as was necessary for the better forming a Theatrical Representation.

It was a very particular Happiness, that I met with a Gentleman so excellently qualify'd as Signor *Rossi*, to fill up the Model I had drawn, with Words so sounding, and so rich in Sense, that if my Translation is in many Places to deviate, 'tis for want of Power to reach the Force of his Original.

Mr. Hendel, whom the World so justly celebrates, has made his Musick speak so finely for its self, that I am purposely silent on that Subject; and shall only add, That as when I undertook this Affair, I had no Gain on the View, but That of the Acknowledgement and Approbation of the Gentlemen of my Country; so No Loss, the Loss of That excepted, shall discourage me from a Pursuit of all Improvements, which can be introduc'd upon our *English* Theatre.

Appendix Two[419]

Works Produced at the Royal Academy of Music.
In order of production. (Not including revivals).

Opera / pasticcio	Composer / adaptations	Librettists	Earlier Text Sources
1719–20			
Numitore	Porta	Rolli	(?)
Radamisto	Handel	Haym	Dominico Lalli on an earlier setting of Gasparini
Narciso	D.Scarlatti with arias by Roseingrave	Rolli	Zeno
1720–1721			
Astarto	Bononcini	Rolli	Zeno and Pietro Pariati

---

[419] Information for opera listings in the Appendices are based on Deutsch, op. cit., and Carole Taylor's season listings in her thesis *Italian Operagoing*, pp. 340–353.

Arsace	Amadei (adapted from Orlandini)	Rolli	Salvi
Muzio Scevola	Amadei, Bononcini, Handel	Rolli	(?)
Ciro	Bononcini	Rolli	Burney attributed the opera to Ariosti
1721–1722			
Floridante	Handel	Rolli	(?)
Crispo	Bononcini	Rolli	Gaetano Lemer
Griselda	Bononcini	Rolli	Zeno
1722–1723			
Ottone	Handel	Haym	Stefano Benedetto Pallavicino
Coriolano	Ariosti	Haym	by Haym (?)
Erminia	Bononcini	Rolli	(?)
Flavio	Handel	Haym	Partly adapted

			from Pierre Corneille's *Le Cid* & altered from Stefano Ghigi.
1723–1724			
Farnace	Bononcini	Bononcini (?)	(?)
Vespasiano	Ariosti	Haym	by Haym (?)
Giulio Cesare	Handel	Haym	(?)
Calfurnia	Bononcini	Haym	(?)
Aquilio Consolo	Ariosti	Haym	Chrysander attributes this opera to Ariosti
1724–1725			
Tamerlano	Handel	Haym	Agostino Piovene
Artaserse	Ariosti	Haym	Zeno and Pariati
Rodelinda	Handel	Haym	Antonio Salvi
Dario	Ariosti	Haym (?)	(?)
Elpida (pasticcio)	Handel; music by Vinci and others	Haym	Zeno

1725–1726			
Elisa (pasticcio)	Porpora (?) Ariosti (?)	Haym (?)	(?)
Scipione	Handel	Rolli	Zeno
Alessandro	Handel	Rolli	Rolli; an original
1726–1727			
Lucio Vero	Ariosti	Haym (?)	(?)
Admeto	Handel	Rolli (?) Haym (?)	Aurelio Aurelli
Astianatte	Bononcini	Haym	Salvi
1727–1728			
Teuzzone (adaptation)	Ariosti (?)	Haym (?)	Zeno
Riccardo Primo	Handel	Rolli	(?)
Siroe	Handel; Vinci (?)	Haym	Metastasio
Tolomeo	Handel	Haym	(?)
1728–			

1729: no season offered.			

Appendix Three

Second Royal Academy Seasons managed
by Handel and Heidegger.

In order of production. (Not including revivals).

Opera / Pasticcio	Composer / adaptation	Librettists	Earlier Text Sources
1729–1730			
Lotario	Handel	(?)	Salvi, set by Giuseppe Maria Orlandini
Partenope	Handel	(?)	Stampiglia
Ormisda (pasticcio)	Handel; from Vinci, Hasse, and others	(?)	Zeno
1730–1731			
Vinceslao (pasticcio)	Handel; from Vinci, Hasse	Humphreys	Zeno
Poro	Handel	Humphreys	Metastasio

1731–1732			
Ezio	Handel	Humphreys	Metastasio
Sosarme	Handel	Humphreys	Matteo Noris
Esther (oratorio)	Handel	Pope	
Lucio Papirio (pasticcio)	Handel; from Frugoni, Antonio Caldara	(?)	Zeno
Acis and Galatea (masque)	Handel	Gay	
1732– 1733			
Catone in Utica (pasticcio)	Handel; from Leonardo Leo (?)	Humphreys	Metastasio
Orlando	Handel	Humphreys	Grazio Braccioli (?)
Deborah (oratorio)	Handel	Humphreys	
Athalia (oratorio) Perfomed at Oxford	Handel	Humphreys	

Appendix Four

Handel and the Opera of the Nobility.
In order of production. (Not including revivals).[420]

Work	Composer / adaptation	Librettists	Earlier Text Sources
1733–34			
Handel (King's Theatre)			
Semiramide (pasticcio)	Handel; from Vinci, others,	(?)	Metastasio
Cajo Fabricio (pasticcio)	Handel; Hasse, others,	(?)	Zeno
Arbaces (pasticcio)	Handel; Vinci (?)	(?)	Metastasio
Arianna in Creta	Handel; Pariati,	(?)	Arranged by Francis Colman (?)

---

[420] With the exception of *Ottone*, revived by the Opera of the Nobility company.

Il Parnasso in Festa (serenata)	Handel	(?)	(?)
The Opera of the Nobility (Lincoln's–Inn–Fields)			
Arianna in Nasso	Porpora	Rolli	by Rolli (?)
Ferdinando	Porpora	(?)	(?)
David e Bersabea (oratorio)	Porpora	Rolli	
Belmira (pasticcio)	(?)	(?)	(?)
Aeneas	Porpora	Rolli	(?)
1734–1735			
Handel (Covent Garden)			

Terpsichore (dramatic entertainment) added to *Il Pastor Fido*.	Handel	Rossi	Quarini
Oreste (self-pasticcio)	Handel	(?)	(?)
Ariodante	Handel	(?)	Salvi
Alcina	Handel	(?)	A. Marchi
The Opera of the Nobility (King's Theatre)			
Artaserse	Hasse and R. Broschi	(?)	(?)
Ottone (revival)	Handel (!)	Haym	Pallavicino
Polifemo	Porpora	Rolli	(?)
Issipile	P. Sandoni	Corri	Metastasio
Iphigenia in Aulide	Porpora	Rolli	(?)

1735–1736			
Handel (Covent Garden)			
Alexander's Feast (ode)	Handel	Hamilton	Dryden
Atalanta	Handel	(?)	Valeriano
The Opera of the Nobility			
Adriano in Siria	Veracini	Corri	Metastasio
Mitridate (pasticcio)	Porpora	(?)	DaGavardo
Orfeo (pasticcio)	(?)	Rolli	by Rolli (?)
Onorio	F.Campi	D. Lolli and G. Boldoni	(?)

La Festa d'Imeneo	Porpora	Rolli	(?)
1736–1737			
Handel (Covent Garden)			
Arminio	Handel	(?)	Salvi (?)
Giustino	Handel	(?)	N. Beregani
Didone (pasticcio)	Handel; Vinci	(?)	Metastasio
Berenice	Handel	(?)	Salvi
The Opera of the Nobility			
Siroe*	Hasse	(?)	Metastasio
Merope*	Broschi	Hill (?)	Zeno
Demetrio*	Pescetti	(?)	Metastasio

---

*   Featuring these comic interludes as afterpieces; *Il Giocatore, Pourceaugnac, Grullo and Moschetta, Il Impresario, Le Bourgeous.* Taylor, *Italian Operagoing*, pp. 352–353.

La Clemenza di Tito*	Veracini	Corri	Metastasio
Sabrina*	Pescetti; arranged by Rolli (!)	Rolli	on Milton's 'Comus'
Demofoonte	E. Duni	A. Corri	Metastasio

Appendix Five

A satirical attack upon Walpole with
reference to Handel.[421]
(Or vice versa). Possibily written by Rolli.

From the "Craftsman", 7th April 1733

SIR,

I am always rejoiced, when I see a *Spirit of Liberty* exert itself
among any Sett, or Denomination of my Countrymen. I please
myself with the Hopes that it will grow more diffusive; some time
or other become fashionable; and at last useful to the Publick. As I
know your Zeal for *Liberty*, I thought I could not address better
than to you the following exact Account of the noble Stand, lately by
the polite Part of the World, in Defense of their Liberties and
Properties, against the open Attacks and bold Attempts of Mr. H—
l's upon both. I shall singly relate the Fact, and leave you, who are
better able than I am, to make what Inferences, or Applications may
be proper.

The Rise and Progress of Mr. H—l's Power and Fortune are
too well known for me now to relate. Let it suffice to say that He
was grown so insolent upon the sudden and undeserved Increase of
both, that He thought nothing ought to oppose his imperious and
extravagant Will. He had, for some Time, govern'd the *Opera's*, and

---

[421] From Deutsch, pp.310–312, and Dorris, *Italian Circle*, pp. 103–
106.

modell'd the *Orchestre*, without the least Controul. No Voices, no *Instruments* were admitted, but such as flatter'd his Ears, though they shock'd those of the Audience. *Wretched Scrapers* were put above the *best Hands* in the *Orchestre*. No Musick but his *own* was to be allowed, though every Body was weary of it; and he had the Impudence to assert, *that there was no Composer* in England *but Himself.* Even *Kings* and *Queens* were to be content with whatever low Characters he was pleased to assign them, as it was evident in the case of Signior *Montagnana*; who, though a *King,* is always obliged to act (except an angry, rumbling Song or two) the most insignificant Part of the whole Drama. This Excess and Abuse of Power soon disgusted the Town; his Government grew odious; and his *Opera's* grew empty. However, this Degree of Unpopularity and general Hatred, instead of humbling him, only made him more furious and desperate. He resolved to make one last Effort to establish his Power and Fortune by Force, since He found it now impossible to hope for it from the good Will of Mankind. In order to This, he form'd a Plan, without consulting any of his *Friends,* (if he has any) and declared that at a proper Season he wou'd communicate it to the Publick; assuring us, at the same Time, that it would be very much for the Advantage of the Publick in general, and his *Opera's* in particular. Some People suspect that he settled it previously with the Signora *Strada del Po,* who is much more in his Favour; but all, that I can advance with certainty, is that He had concerted it with a *Brother of his own,* in whom he places a most undeserved Confidence. In this Brother of his, *Heat* and *Dullness* are miraculously united. The *former* prompts him to any Thing new and violent; while the *latter* hinders him from seeing any of the Inconveniences of it. As Mr. H—l's *Brother,* he thought it necessary he should be a Musician too, but all he could arrive at, after a very laborious Application for many years, was a moderate Performance upon the *Jew's Trump.* He had, for some Time, play'd *a parte buffa* abroad, and had entangled his *Brother* in several troublesome and dangerous Engagements, in the Commissions he had given them to contract with *foreign Performers*; and from which (by the way) Mr.

H—l did not disengage Himself with much Honour. Notwithstanding all these and many more Objections, Mr. H—l, by and with the advice of *his Brother*, at last produces his *Project*, resolves to cram it down the Throats of the Town; prostitutes *great and aweful Names*, as the Patrons of it; and even does not scruple to insinuate that they are not to be the Sharers of the Profit. His *Scheme* set forth in Substance, that the late Decay of *Opera's* was owing to their *Cheapness*, and to the great *Frauds* committed by the *Doorkeepers*; that the *annual Subscribers* were a Parcel of *Rogues*, and made ill Use of their Tickets, by *running* two into the Gallery, that to obviate these Abuses he had contrived a Thing, that was better than an *Opera*, call'd an *Oratorio;* to which none should be admitted, but by *printed Permits*, or Tickets of one Guinea each, which should be distributed out of *Warehouses of his own*, and by *Officers of his own naming;* which *Officers* would not so reasonably be supposed to cheat in the Collection of *Guineas*, as the *Doorkeepers* in the collection of *half-Guineas;* and lastly; that as the very being of *Opera's* depended upon *Him singly*, it was just that the Profit arising from hence should be for his *own Benefit*. He has added, indeed, one Condition, to varnish the whole a little; which was, that if any Person should think himself aggriev'd, and that the *Oratorio* was not worth the Price of the *Permitt*, he should be at Liberty to appeal to *three Judges of Music*, who should be oblig'd, within the Space of seven Years at farthest, finally to determine the same; provided always that the said *Judges* should be of his Nomination, and known to like no other Musick but his.

The Absurdity, Extravagancy, and Opposition of this *Scheme* disgusted the whole Town. Many of the most constant Attenders of the *Opera's* resolved absolutely to renounce them, rather than go to them under such Extortion and Vexation. They exclaim'd against the *insolent and rapacious Projector of this Plan*. The King's old and sworn Servants of the two Theatres of *Drury-Lane* and *Covent-Garden* reap'd the Benefit of this general Discontent, and were resorted to in Crowds, by the way of Opposition to the *Oratorio*. Even the fairest Breasts were fir'd with Indignation against this *new*

Imposition. Assemblies, Cards, Tea, Coffee, and all other Female Batteries were vigorously employ'd to defeat the *Project,* and destroy the *Projector.* These joint Endeavours of all Ranks and Sexes succeeded so well, that the *Projector* had the Mortification to see but a very thin audience in his *Oratorio*; and of about two hundred and sixty odd, that it consisted of, it was notorious that not ten paid for their *Permits,* but, on the contrary, had given them, and Money into the Bargain, for coming to keep him in Countenance.

This Accident, they say, has thrown Him into a *deep Melancholy,* interrupted sometimes by *raving Fits*; in which he fancies he sees ten thousand *Opera* Devils coming to tear Him to Pieces; then He breaks out into frantic, incoherent Speeches; muttering *sturdy Beggars, Assassination,* &c. In these delirious Moments, he discovers a particular Aversion to the City. He calls them a Parcel of *Rogues,* and asserts that the *honest trader among them deserves to be hang'd* — It is much question'd whether he will recover; at least, if he does, it is not doubted but He will seek for a Retreat in his *own Country* from the general Resentment of the Town.

I am Sir, Sir,

Your very humble Servant,

O.   P—LO   R—LI.

P.S. Having seen a little Epigram, lately handed about Town, which seems to allude to the same Subject, I believe it will not be unwelcome to your Readers.

EPIGRAM

Quoth *W—e* {Walpole} to *H—l,* Shall We Two agree,
And exise the whole Nation?

H. si, Caro, si.

Of what Use are *Sheep,* if the *Shepherd* can't shear them?

At the *Hay-Market* I, you at *Westminster.*

W. Hear Him!

Call'd to Order, their *Seconds* appear in Place;

One fam'd for his *Morals,* and one for his *Face.***

In half They succeeded, in half They were crost:

The EXISE was obtain'd, but poor DEBORAH lost.

O.

** "The two seconds = the dissolute Lord Hervey and the ugly Heidegger." Hogwood, *Handel,* f. on p. 104.

Appendix Six

From the article by Milhous and Hume, 'Handel's Opera Finances in 1732-33.'[422]

An excerpt from the new MS now housed
in the Rare Book Room,
Pennsylvania State University

[f. 2r]

Strada

```
1732/3 March 1 - - paid Signora Strada on Account -- 200
1733  - -    28  p̶a̶i̶d̶ ̶D̶i̶t̶t̶o̶ ̶m̶o̶r̶e̶ ̶b̶y̶ ̶P̶a̶y̶m̶e̶n̶t̶ ̶t̶o̶ ̶M̶r̶.̶ ̶P̶o̶t̶t̶e̶r̶   Att
                 b̶y̶ ̶h̶e̶r̶ ̶o̶r̶d̶e̶r̶                            3̶0̶:̶4̶
         April 6 -- paid ditto more on Account --                 12:12
         J̶u̶l̶y̶ ̶9̶ 11 -- paid Ditto more on Account --                157:10
         July 9 - - p̶a̶i̶d̶ ̶D̶i̶t̶t̶o̶ ̶m̶o̶r̶e̶ ̶b̶y̶ ̶p̶a̶y̶m̶e̶n̶t̶ ̶t̶o̶ ̶M̶r̶
                 P̶o̶t̶t̶e̶r̶ ̶b̶y̶ ̶O̶r̶d̶e̶r̶                       1̶5̶:̶2̶
              25 - - paid Ditto more on Account - -               100:00
         September 27 paid Ditto more on Account - -    50:00
                                                    _____
                                                       £565:8
         paid Extra singers £                                     21:0
                                               586:8:0
              Arrears remaining due to ye 2 Undertakers
              for ye 1st 2d 3d & 4th seasons of Operas as follows
```

---

[422] I have reproduced the excerpt of the MS as it is in the article as close as possible. Milhous and Hume have expanded most abbreviations, lowered superscript letters and regularized the format for the sake of clarity.

In 1st Season

On subscription From Henry Davenant Esquire   10:10:0
honourable James Brudenell Esquire   15:15:0   26:5:0

In 2d Season
On subscription From Henry Davenant Esquire   10:10:0
honourable James Brudenell Esquire   15:15:0
26:5:0
side Boxes -- Sir Herbot Peckington 42   88:4:0   133:7:0
Lord Bingley 9 Nights   18:18:0
107:2:0

In 3d season
On subscription From William Bumpsted Esquire   15:15
Sir Robert Hessly   15:15
31:10:0
side Boxes Dutchess of Buckingham 21 Nights 44:2:0   075:12:0
£44:2:0

In 4th season
On subscription From honourable James Brudenell
Esquire   15:15:0
William Fisher Esquire   15:15:0
Earle of Staire   15:15:0
Monsieur De Wynd   15:15:0
63:0:0
Side Boxes -- Dutchess of Newcastle 50 Nights   105:0:0
Dutchess of Buckingham 20   42:0:0
Lady Ann Hamilton   52:10:0
Lord Carnarvan 1   02: 2:0
201:12
264:12:0
£499:16:0

730:2:0
63:11:0

793:13:0

2940:0
[f.2v]   5359:7:9
5301:6:8

58:1:1

237

Appendix Seven[423]

Dedication by John Rich (1726)
to the *Rape of Proserpine*

Though my Inclinaton to Musick frequently leads me to visit the *Italian* Opera; yet, I confess, it is not in the Power of the present excellent Performers to prevent my falling into the very common Opinion, that there are many essential Requisites still wanting, to establish that Entertainment on a lasting Foundation, and to adapt it to the Taste of an *English* Audience.

For, not to mention the trite Objection of the Performance being in Italian, and the general ill Choice of the Subjects for those Compositions, it is evident, that the vast Expence of procuring foreign Voices, does necessarily exclude those various Embellishments of Machinery, Painting, Dances, as well as Poetry itself, which have been always esteemed (except till very lately in *England*) Auxiliaries absolutely necessary to the Success of Musick; and, without which, it cannot be long supported, unless by very great Subscriptions, of which we naturally grow tired in a few Years.

It seems, therefore, the only Way by which Musick can be established in England, is to give it Assistances from other Arts which it yet wants, and by that Means to adapt it still more to the Publick Taste; to moderate, as much as possible, the Expense of it, and thereby make it a general Diversion, which hitherto it has not

---

[423] John Rich, dedication to *The Rape of Proserpine: as it is Acted at the Theatre Royal in Lincoln's-Inn-Fields. Written by Theobald, and Set to Musick by Mr. Galliard*, 5th ed. (London: T. Wood, 1731): iii–vi. Copy used; British Library, Reference Division 11775.c.87, in McCleave, *Dance in Handel's Operas*, pp. 60–62.

been.

You will perceive, Sir, that in the following Entertainment, the Vocal Parts of which are here presented to you, I have endeavoured to introduce that Variety which has usually been thought agreeable on the Stage and have attempted to form the serious part of it upon the above-mentioned Plan, as a Specimen of what may not be displeasing to the English Audience, and from which the Town may be able to form a Judgement of the Effect an Opera would have, if conducted (by an abler Hand) in the same Manner.

As for the other Parts, it might, perhaps, seem an Affectation in me to detain you with the History of the ancient Pantomime Entertainments, or to make a long Apology for the Revival of them at present. This much, however, may be said in their Favour, that this Theatre has of late owed its Support in a great Measure to them. I own myself extremely indebted to the Favour with which the Town is pleased to receive my Attempts to entertain them in this Kind, and do engage, for my own Part, that whenever the Publick Taste shall be disposed to return to the Works of the *Drama*, no one shall rejoice more sincerely than myself.

Example 1: *Giulio Cesare:* "V' adoro," Bars 1–7, 40–47, and recitative. *Giulio Cesare.* Kalmus Minature Score Series, No. 1269. New York: Edwin F. Kalmus, pp. 56, 58.

Example 2: *Tamerlano:* "Se potessi un di placare," Bars 1–28. *Tamerlane.* Kalmus Miniature Score Series, No. 1291. New York: Edwin F. Kalmus, p. 86.

Example 3: *Oreste:* "Coro di popolo e Sinfonia". *Oreste; opera in tre atti,* HWV A[11]. Hallische Händel–Ausgabe edition, Kritische Gesamtausgabe, Bärenreiter Kassel, BA 4045, (1991), pp. 126–127.

Example 4: *Ariodante:* Act II, Scene I Sinfonia. *Ariodante.* Kalmus Minature Score Series, No. 1261. New York: Edwin F. Kalmus, p. 62.

Example 5: *Ariodante:* "Prendi da questo mano," Bars 80–84. *Ariodante.* Kalmus Minature Score Series, No. 1261. New York: Edwin F. Kalmus, p. 22.

Example 6: *Ariodante:* Act II Finale recitative. *Alcina.* (sic.) Kalmus Minature Score Series, No.1255. New York: Edwin F. Kalmus, p. 107.

Bibliography

Abraham, Gerald. ed. *Handel: a Symposium.* London: Oxford University Press, 1954.

Brett, Philip and Haggerty, George. 'Handel and the Sentimental; the Case of *Athalia.*' *Music and Letters* vol 68, no. 2 (1987): pp. 112–127.

Burrows, D. ed. *The Cambridge Companion to Handel,* Cambridge University Press, 1997.

Chapman, Clive. 'Sir, it will not Do! John Rich and Covent Garden's Early Years.' *Music and Letters,* vol. 123 (1982): pp. 831–835.

Cudworth, Charles. 'Handel and the French Style.' *Music and Letters,* 40 (1959): pp. 122–131.

Cummings, Graham. 'Handel's Compositional Methods in his London Operas of the 1730s, and the Unusual Case of *Poro, Rè dell'Indie* (1731).' *Music and Letters* vol. 79, no. 3 (1998): pp. 346–367.

Dean, Winton.

– 'Charles Jennen's Marginalia to Mainwaring's Life of Handel.' *Music and Letters* vol. 53, No. 2   (April,1972): pp. 160–166.

– *Handel and the Opera Seria.* United States: University of California Press Ltd., 1969.

– and Merrill Knapp, John. *Handel's Operas;1704–1726.* Oxford: Clarendon Press, 1987.

Deutsch, Otto Erich. *Handel; a Documentary Biography.* New York: Da Capo Press, 1974.

Dorris, George, E. *Paolo Rolli and the Italian Circle in London.* The Hague: Mounton and Co., 1967.

Flower, Newman. *Handel; His Personality and his Times.* London: Granada Publishing Ltd, 1923, 1959. Reprint, 1972. Harris, Ellen T. *Handel and the Pastoral Tradition.* London: Oxford University Press, 1980.

Hogwood, Christopher. *Handel.* New York, Thames and Hudson Inc., 1984. Reprint; 1995.

Hume, Robert D. 'Handel and Opera Management in London in the 1730s.' *Music and Letters* vol. 67 no. 4 (October, 1986): pp. 347–362.

Knapp, Merril. 'A Forgotten Chapter in English Eighteenth-Century Opera.' *Music and Letters* vol. XLII, (1961): pp. 4–16.

Landon, H. C. Robbins. *Handel and His World.* London, Glasgow: Flamingo Edition, HarperCollins, 1984. Reprint, 1992.

Larue, C. Stephen. *Handel and his Singers; The Creation of the Royal Academy Operas, 1720–1728.* Oxford; Clarendon Press, 1995.

Lindgren, Lowell. 'The Accomplishments of the Learned and Ingenious Nicola Francesco Haym (1678–1729).' *Studi Musicali,* Anno XVI – No. 2. (Firenze,1987): pp. 247–380.

Lowens, Irving. 'The *Touch-Stone* (1728); A Neglected View of London Opera.' *The Musical Quarterly* 45 (1959): pp. 325–342.

McCleave, Sarah, Y. *Dance in Handel's Italian Operas: The Collaboration with Marie Sallé*, PH.D. University of London, King's College, 1993.

McGeary, Thomas. 'Handel, Prince Frederick, and the Opera of the Nobility Reconsidered.' *GöttingerHändel–Beiträge* 7 (1998): pp. 156–178.

Mainwaring, John. *Memoirs of the Life of the Late George Frederic Handel*. London: R. And J. Dodsley, in *PallMall*, 1760. Reprint, New York: Da Capo Press Music Reprint Series, 1980.

Mathews, Betty. 'Unpublished Letters Concerning Handel.' *Music and Letters* vol. XL, no. 2 (1959): pp. 261–268.

Milhous, Judith. 'Opera Finances in London; 1674–1738.' *Journal of the American Musicological Society* vol. XXXVII, no. 3 (1984): pp. 567–592.

Milhous, Judith and Hume, Robert D.

– 'Handel's Opera Finances in 1732–33.' *Musical Times* 125 (1984): pp. 86–89.

– 'J.F. Lampe and English Opera at the Little Haymarket in 1732-33.' *Music and Letters*, vol. 78, No. 4 (November, 1997): pp. 502–532.

– 'New Light on Handel and The Royal Academy of Music in 1720.' *Theatre Journal* XXV (1983): pp. 149–167.

Roberts, John H. 'Handel and Vinci's *Didone abbandonata*; Revisions and Borrowings.' *Music and Letters* vol. 68, no 2 (1987): pp. 141–150.

Raguenet, François. 'A Comparison Between the French and Italian Music.' *The Musical Quaterly* vol. XXXII, No. 3 (July, 1946): pp. 411–436.

Schueller, Herbert M. ' "Imitation" and "Expression" in British Music Criticism in the 18th Century.' *MusicalQuarterly* vol. XXXIV, no. 4 (1948): pp. 544–565.

Shapiro, Alexander H. ' "Drama of an Infinitely Superior Nature:" Handel's Early Oratorios and the Religious Sublime.' *Music and Letters* vol 74, no. 2 (1993): pp. 215–245.

Smith, William C. 'More Handeliana.' *Music and Letters*   vol. XXXIV no. 1 (January, 1953): pp. 11–24.

Smith, Ruth. *Handel's Oratorios and Eighteenth-Century Thought.* Cambridge University Press, 1995.

Stanley, S. ed. and Hicks, A. ed. *Handel; TercentenaryCollection.* Hong Kong: Macmillan Press Ltd., 1987.

Strohm, Reinhard.

   – *Dramma per Musica: Italian Opera Seria of the Eighteenth Century.* New Haven, London: Yale   University Press, 1997.

   – *Essay's on Handel and Italian Opera.* Great Britain: Cambridge University Press, 1985.

Taylor, Carole.

    – PH.D. Thesis. *Italian Operagoing in London,1700–1745.* Syracuse University, 1991.

    – 'Handel and Frederick, Prince of Wales.' *Musical Times* 125 (1984): pp. 89–92.

Westrup, J. A. 'Purcell and Handel.' *Music and Letters* vol. XL, no. 2 (1959): pp. 103–108.

White, Eric Walter. *A History of English Opera.* London: Faber and Faber Ltd., BAS Printers. Ltd., 1983.

Williams, Peter. ed. *Bach, Handel Scarlatti; Tercentenary Essays.* Cambridge: Cambridge University Press, 1985.

Scores:
George Fridrick Handel

Aci, Galatea, e Polofemo, Serenata di G.F. Handel. Kalmus Miniature Score Series, No. 1295. New York: Edwin F. Kalmus.

Alcina. Kalmus Minature Score Series, No.1255. New York: Edwin F. Kalmus.

Alessando. Kalmus Miniature Score Series, No. 1256. New York: Edwin F. Kalmus.

Ariodante. Kalmus Miniature Score Series, No. 1261. New York: Edwin F. Kalmus.

Giulio Cesare. Kalmus Miniature Score Series, No. 1269. New York: Edwin F. Kalmus.

Oreste; opera in tre atti, HWV A[11]. Hallische Händel–Ausgabe edition, Kritische Gesamtausgabe, Bärenreiter   Kassel, BA 4045, (1991).

Al Parnasso in Festa; Serenata. Kalmus Miniature Score Series, No. 1304. New York: Edwin F. Kalmus.

Radamisto. Kalmus Minature Score Series, No. 1280. New York: Edwin F. Kalmus.

Rodrigo. Kalmus Miniature Score Series, No. 1285. New York: Edin F. Kalmus.

Tamerlane. Kalmus Miniature Score Series, No. 1291. New York: Edwin F. Kalmus.

Terpsicore and *Il Pastor Fido Second version*, 1734. Kalmus Miniature Score Series, no. 1278. New York: Edwin F. Kalmus.

A Select Index

247

251

254

Lightning Source UK Ltd.
Milton Keynes UK
UKOW040635131112

202094UK00003B/34/P